Jan Fries
Visual Magick

Mandrake of Oxford

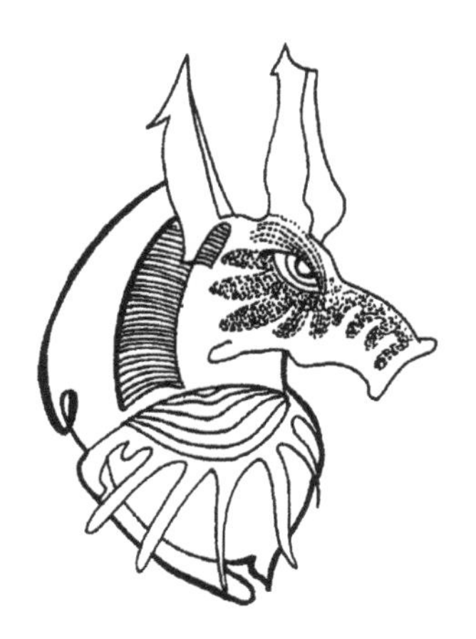

Visual Magick

A practical guide to trance, sigils and visualization techniques

Jan Fries

By the Same Author
Helrunar: a manual of rune magick
Seidways: shaking, swaying and serpent mysteries
Living Midnight: three movements of the Tao

I would like to acknowledge to help of Custor and Mouse in the preparation of this manuscript for publication

Fries, Jan
Visual Magick
1. Magic (Occultism)
I. Titles
133.43
ISBN 978-1-869928-57-5

Preface

I was amazed, and highly flattered, when asked to write this preface. I knew Jan only slightly, though my wife (Nema) had been corresponding with him for some years. But, in the three days since I had met him in the flesh I had seen sides of him at work and at play that I have seen in few others. I would like to think that he had seen the same in me. He is my brother.

I was unsure what to say at first. I wanted to share with the readers the wild, unfettered spirit that leaped and danced on our English tour. But I decided that that was impossible.

I can say that Jan represents, to me, a model of a modern magician, one that would capture the fancy of Aleister Crowley, were he alive today. For Jan is doing original research, exploring new pathways, not content to repeat the work of generations gone by. More important, he is communicating the results of his work in a highly readable and entertaining form.

This book is important for several reasons. First and foremost, it is Pan-Aeonic. That is, it draws on a variety of sources using a variety of Aeonic formulae (See *Cincinnati Journal* number seven for more on Pan-Aeonic Magick). Jan's main emphasis draws on the most ancient shamanic techniques of paleolithic Europe. The difference between this book and other shamanic texts is that Jan does not hold himself just to traditional teachings. He includes techniques from Crowley and even more modern writers. He also analyses Magick in terms of the most recent psychological models.

Second, nothing is (overly) sacred to Jan. He has maintained an ability to laugh that has been ground out of many Magicians by the time they have reached his level of awareness. The attitude of playfulness that Jan projects, even in writing, makes reading this book a true delight.

Third, Jan has an attitude of skepticism. He does not consider himself the final authority on anything. He dares the reader to find new and better methods that he has never considered. If you prefer to practise rote exercises as taught by a perfect master, find another book.

Last, and possibly most important, Jan urges you to explore (and explore with) your body. Too many magicians are of the armchair sort, reading and analyzing, or sitting in meditation or scrying. Jan's Magick is of the arm-swinging, twirling, climb-the-tree active form of magick. If you don't like to feel out of breath, you are advised to find other texts.

Now the reader has been told about the book and must judge for themselves whether it is worth the time and money. I can only hope so.

Mike Ingalls

Contents

Ganesha, Breaker of Obstacles

Chapter One
The Seed

A seed is a unit of consciousness that has body, charge and intelligence and tends to develop from potential into the actual under proper conditions. Seeds are created, transmitted and earthed in order to achieve change—change in one's world, life or identity.

Seeds may have many shapes, according to the will and nature of the magician. They may be visual, as sigils; or acoustic, as tunes, Chaos song or mantra; they may be physical, such as the chance objects found in the wild on shamanic journeys; or may find their form in dance, gesture, ritual or event-experience. We will treat the seed's development in the language of sigil magick in this book. Consider that sigils are just one variety of seed, and that the basic principles can easily be applied to some other medium.

How is the sigil made?

First, we have to consider what we want. At this stage it is not always easy to determine whether the desire is an aspect of the true will or whether it expresses some egoistic need. In the latter case, the sigil will not realize; in the former, it will attach itself to the subconscious force-stream of the universal will, and manifestation is just a matter of time. Basically, sigils can be made for all kinds of desire.

All desire, whether for pleasure, knowledge, or power, that cannot find 'natural' expression, can by sigils and their formula find fulfilment from the subconsciousness.

A O Spare, The Book of Pleasure.

There are several methods of constructing sigils; the oldest of them is probably the shamanic method. A shaman might go out into the wilderness to find the tools for some specific sorcery. Concentrating on his aim and singing power songs, he will travel in a trance state as the spirits lead him, and collect all objects that catch his attention in a special way. Some of them might be used for some symbolic meaning, while others would carry no meaning at all; that is, to the reasoning mind.

These items would be gathered, blessed, joined and buried in a special place. Examples of such practices come from Seeland. In Maglehoi, a bronze vessel was unearthed that contained the following items: horse teeth, weasel bones, the claw of a lynx, the spine of a serpent, the windpipe of a small bird, diverse bone splinters, remnants of a rowan twig, pebbles with sulphur, coal, and some bits of bronze.

In Lyngby, Seeland, a leather bag was uncovered containing a serpent tail, the claw of a falcon, a shell from the Mediterranean, a flint arrow-tip, a piece of amber, stones wrapped in a bladder and a small leather bag containing a squirrel's jawbones.

Both of these collections are dated between 1000-800 BC. The Celtic tribes had a similar custom. They used to dig deep shafts into the earth and fill them with several layers of earth, stones, bones, ritual objects, corpses, stag horns, sacrificial gifts, etc., until no trace of the former hole remained. The various layers were filled according to some regular pattern the meaning of which can only be guessed at nowadays.

The sigil as a visual device can be traced to the Paleolithic period. Many complicated sigils were drawn by our Stone Age ancestors, sigils that defy interpretation, as they are too abstract for symbols, and too complicated for letters.

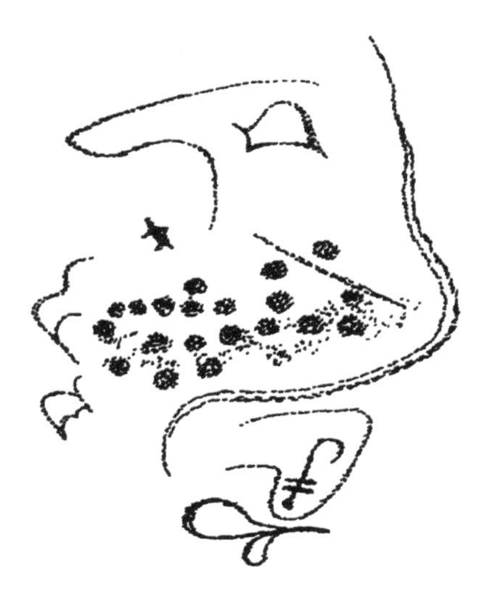

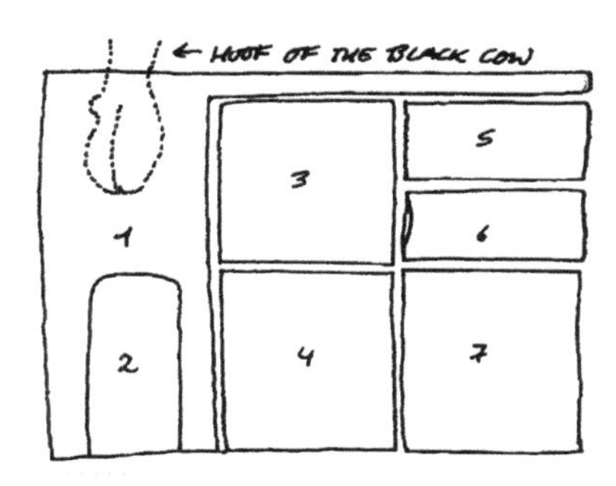

***Left:** Peche-Merle cave, France. Sigils in red ochre on the ceiling of the cave. **Right:** Lascaux cave. One of the curious coloured squares under the hoofs of the 'Black Cow'. As far as could be deduced from three photos, the colouring is as follows: 1. Greenish black 2. Brownish black 3. Rich red ochre 4. Light ochre (sand colour/cream) 5. Dark sand colour 6. Grey/black 7. Dark red ochre. The lines between the fields are in white chalk. (I hope you like riddles.)*

Medieval sigils should be familiar from the various grimoires. The desire—in this case, the name of some Spirit or Intelligence—was written out in the Hebrew alphabet. Each letter was then changed into a number, and the whole series of numbers was written as a continuous line into one of the Magical Squares. Details of this method are given in Israel Regardie's *How to Make and Use Talismans*, or his monumental *Golden Dawn System of Magick*.

4	9	2
3	5	7
8	1	6

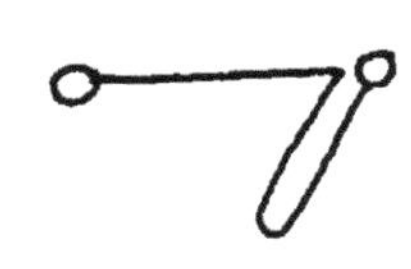

Example: The sigil of Zazel, Spirit of Saturn, is written on the square of Saturn (3x3). Zazel is spelled as Z(7), A(1), Z(7), E(5), L(30). The 30 is modified into 3, as the square is too small for the full number.

Rune magicians had their own method of sigilizing. One of them is called 'Binderunen', and functions much like Austin Spare's method. They would write their desire in Rune letters, and combine these into a single glyph. An example. 'Wodan' might be written as:

·ᚹᛟᛞᚨᚾ· = OR

Another method made use of the three 'Aettir' ('Family' or 'Eight') into which the Rune alphabets are divided.

The position of each Rune determines the code.

ᚠ is the 1st of the 1st Aettir,
ᛦ the 7th of the 2nd,
ᛞ the 4th of the 3rd, etc.

If you wish to write < for instance, you might codify it as: ·ı||||||· ie first Aettir (the small rune), sixth letter. Or ·ᚾᛉᛉᛉᛉᛉᛉ·
Another code used the fir shape:

= ·|· (2. AETTIR, 3. RUNE).

There were several codes based on this method, such as the fish code, the face code and several other varieties:

In some cases, a whole word might be shaped like a wheel. This example would spell ᛁᛞᚢᚾ - IDUN (more on rune magick in my book *Helrunar*.)

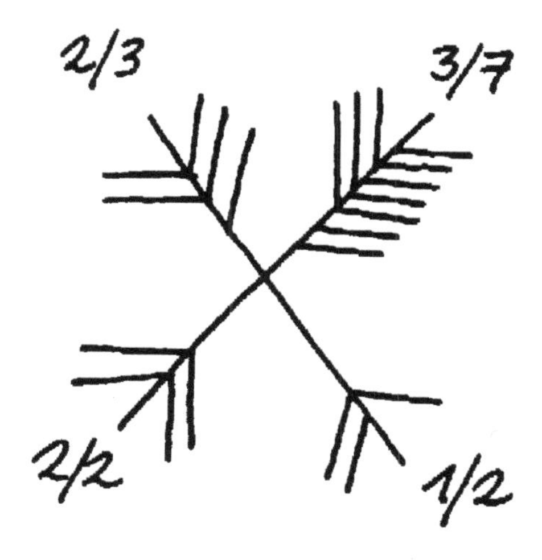

The new area of sigil magick began with the popularization of Austin Spare's method. This system is quite simple and suitable for all kinds of purposes. We begin by writing our desire in a clear and concise shape, be it as a sentence, or, better still, as a single word. If we desire 'endurance', for instance, we would first get rid of all double letters.

This leaves us with 'ENDURAC'. These letters would then be combined to form a pleasant glyph, such as:

You may simplify or elaborate the structure as you feel like it. This system may be refined by the use of a magical alphabet. Ask your 'deep mind' for a system of writing suitable to you, then combine the letters and create a suitable glyph out of them.

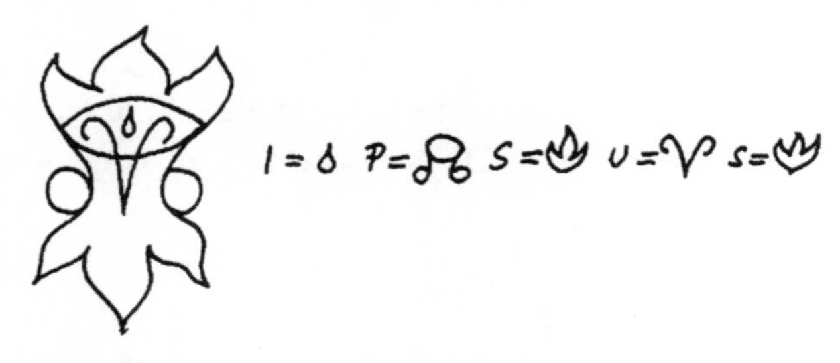

A unique method is suggested by Frater Custor in his magazine *Phoenix Rising* (Vol 1. no 2). Here the desire is vividly imagined until the magician feels aglow with it. Then, while focusing on the desire, the magician begins to cover a sheet of paper with wild, spontaneous ('automatic') drawing. Details of this sort of artwork can be found in a later chapter. When you have covered the paper, close your eyes and concentrate strongly on your desire. Relax.

> *Only when fully relaxed and not until then, take the paper out and look directly at what has been drawn. The very first part of it that catches the eye should be encircled and the rest of the drawing obliterated. Take a fresh piece of paper and reproduce the encircled portion of the original paper at the top of this one. Now repeat the whole process again.*

The procedure is repeated time and time again until one arrives at a sigil that intuitively feels right. The process of developing a suitable sigil is already part of the working, so don't be lazy, and continue, even if it takes several dozen sheets of paper. With practice, one will grow familiar with certain fundamental sigil aesthetics. The advantage of this system lies in the fact that one asks one's 'deep mind' for a glyph in a 'language' easily understood by it. The final result may be simplified. Here are two examples. (The purpose escapes me).

There is a curious similarity between sigils produced in the method mentioned above and the sigils used by left-hand Taoism to evoke the six Chia Spirits. The sigil given here is used to evoke the Chia-Tzu Spirit called Huang-Chen. The sigil is drawn with the brush on paper—this sort of linework is quite difficult with a brush—and with the sword in the air. All Chia Spirits correspond to the Chakras, and are their negative or Qliphotic reflections. Details on this system of Magick can be found in Michael Saso's *The Teachings of Taoist Master Chuang.*

Another method of sigil crafting consists of writing the desire in a continuous line, but not in the proper linear fashion. Form the letters as they come, on top of each other, or pointing any way that happens. This is 'Power'. You simply fill in the centre of the form, resulting in an indecipherable, amorphous thing.

There is a variety of sigils that should also be mentioned. Until now, we have dealt with sigils that were designed consciously for a specific purpose. Some sigils, however, are not designed but received.

This is the case when we meet a spirit, god, or astral entity and ask for a suitable sigil to describe and evoke it. Such sigils are frequently incomprehensible to our waking mind. We receive them and take them along into our realm of manifest reality, so that the entity from which they came may have easier access to this plane. In a sense, these sigils become the manifest aspect of an unmanifest intelligence; they create a connection between the planes and allow an easier circulation of energy. Examples of this sort of sigil are the ones given in Kenneth Grant's *Nightside of Eden*, or in my own drawings.

It should be noted that, while the sentience behind these sigils appears independent, their aesthetics are usually suited to the personality of the receiver. The best kind contains a blend of known and unknown structures, half revealed and half concealed.

All of these systems have a single idea in common: the sigil should not remind you of the original desire.

The reason for this is simple. Identity, the aspect of self of which you are conscious, is a creature with many desires and many fears. Ego is an agglomeration of habits and beliefs, many of which are in conflict with each other.

If you desire a thing, you have to recognize that this desire is not shared by all aspects of your identity, and that many of your personalities tend to disagree. If you desire money, for instance, parts of your mind will be eager for fulfilment, while others will voice objections or attempt to control the operation.

This is not just 'I want money', pure and simple, but, 'I more or less desire money under such and such conditions.'

'I would not want that money to come to me through some other person's suffering'—this is our ethical self speaking. 'I don't really need much'—here is our humble and modest self. 'The more, the better' comes from our greedy nature. 'I want to work for it'—our dutiful self speaking. 'If I get it, I promise to use it for good ends'—our idealistic identity. 'It won't work anyway'—our cynical nature. 'Don't fool yourself'—the sceptic. 'I'll suspend judgment'—the scientist within. 'I don't care where it's from, as long as it's enough!'—our amoral identity. 'Money is evil'—our pious, spiritual nature. 'Money is necessary!'—our realistic nature. 'It's nice!'—our materialistic identity.

And this is just the beginning. What about the way the desire is fulfilled? Or the possibilities that arise from it? What we considered a single entity—our very own identity—reveals itself as a struggling assortment of personalities, each one of them desperately trying to control the situation and to dominate the rest. Do you think that 'money' is a difficult notion? Think it through with such desires as: magical power; love and affection; changes in identity, if you want to create real trouble.

We are seldom of a single opinion. There is so much struggle and confusion within that we can rarely expect clear action, continuous aims or even internal cooperation, unless a stronger necessity (survival, instinct, or true will) dominates. This is why we employ sigils.

The sigil has a neutral shape. We can work our magick with it without having to consider the 333 internal pros and cons, plus veto rights. We can focus on the shape as it is, ignore its original meaning; and forget about doubts, inhibitions, fears, hopes, desires, needs, necessities, conditions of fulfilment, and all the troublesome rest.

The sigil is abstract in order to avoid conflict or interference by the ego. It is released into the depth, into the realm of true will and pure instinct, and these aspects of the 'inner self' determine how and when manifestation obtains.

The sigil-sorcerer need not concern himself with the question 'is this desire wilful?' We have to accept the fact that we don't always know the nature and motion of will. In a sense, sigil magick is a form of feedback: the desire arises from the deep, is recognized, sigilized, cast into the deep again, and finds fulfilment from that agency.

During the act of transmission, we should avoid thinking of the original desire. Spare advised the creation of several sigils. One sigilizes several desires, then picks one of them at the appropriate time and works with it. It may happen that you have forgotten what the sigils were meant for—this is the ideal state—but at least you might pretend that you forgot, even if the memory arises spontaneously. Pretend that you don't know what it's for: this will produce the necessary attitude of 'friendly indifference' (Spare called it 'union through absent-mindedness') which offers your conscious selves/ego no cause for protest or struggle. All notions of anxiety, necessity, fear, hope, need, lust, etc., are poison to the act of transmission, insofar as they associate the sigil with emotions that inhibit its free passage into the deep.

In the samples given in the Spare's *Book of Pleasure*, he formulates his desires in long sentences: 'This is my wish to obtain the strength of a tiger', for example. I consider this unnecessarily complicated. The 'my wish' can be kicked out—if it weren't my wish I wouldn't sigilize it. The same goes for the 'This', and the 'to obtain'. If we boil it down to 'tiger-strength', we will get a simpler sigil containing less waste material.

Would you tell the acupuncture needle what it is supposed to do? If you stimulate the right point with proper intensity, your subconscious will wake up and correct the situation by restoring the balance. Of course it doesn't look so safe if we sigilize 'Money' instead of 'I desire money'. Can the subconscious mistake our intentions? If the sigil touches the 'money' aspect of our being, true will is sure to know whether addition or subtraction is needed. In this sense, sigil magick is based on trust. Results may appear unpredictable—yet will they be wrong? A sigil is not a command, but a request: we are dealing with intelligence.

The body of the sigil is another important issue. The message can be transmitted more easily if the aesthetics are right. Chinese Taoists, for instance, write their sigils in red ink on yellow paper. The paper may receive the stamp of the sacred seal; half of the sheet may be burned, while the other half is kept.

The use of coloured paper and coloured ink is advisable, provided you have some direct experience with colours and their meaning to you. It is useless to 'look them up' in some book—the knowledge has to come from life. Then, the shape of the paper offers variations. A circle would emphasize the roundness of the seed; a square, the solidity of matter; a triangle express force. It depends on the nature of the desire. Paper is not the only material to be used as a 'body' for your seed.

If material results are intended, some magicians prefer the use of a clay pentacle, the earth being symbolic of body, flesh, reality. Enduring materials—stone, metal, bone—suggest enduring effects. Bone is very good for matters that touch the very core of our being, depending on the associations it raises. If it suggests 'age' or 'essence', you will get along well, but if it suggests 'death and doom' you will need some work on yourself before you can enjoy the material.

Wood is good for all growing things. The Rune magicians used to carve their signs lightly into wood, then they rubbed a little ash or blood over the inscription to make it easier to see. If you use your own blood, this will certainly suggest sincerity and determination.

The metals may be used according to planetary attributions.

Some sigils are only worked in the imagination. The texts of the old Fraternitas Saturni included a number of fairly complicated sigils which were imagined in clear red lines into the full moon disc. If you work in the astral and you find the effort of keeping up a clear vision of your sigil too great, why don't you put it into a seed shape, a treasure chest, a chalice, or some other vessel, and work your will with that?

At times, a temporary body is advisable. If you desire matters of dream magick, you could draw your sigil on paper, fold it into a paper boat, and send it off on a river, stream, or pond. The water destroys the body and receives the idea. You might draw the sigil in earth colours on your skin and dance till you've sweated it off, or form the shape in berries, food for the birds. You could draw it in the earth with a stick and leave it for the rains, or give it, drawn on paper, to the fire. You might even feed on it. Ink can be washed off and drunk with water (use a nontoxic sort), and some sigils can be drawn or baked into cakes or bread. As Nema put it 'Eating is good earthing'.

There are so many ways—do develop some of your own!

Chapter Two
The Ritual

We have created our seed, and are now preparing to plant it in suitable ground. For this purpose we may consider the sigil a message capsule, a unit of form, energy and consciousness that can signal our wishes to the deeper strata of the mind. In one sense the sigil is a message; in another it is a living entity, just as a seed is a potential plant. A third model would consider the sigil as a gateway, a channel that reaches to a related power zone. The sigil is all of these, and more.

The sigil has to be communicated. First, we have to grow familiar with the shape. This means that one knows it well enough to be able to draw it from memory. This is one of the reasons why a sigil should be kept simple and uncomplicated. Some authors insist that the sigil should be so familiar that one can keep its image clear in the imagination for long periods. In my experience, this is not necessary. Familiarity is usually enough—after all, we do give the shape a physical form, and so we may use our eyes and work with that. Clear and continuous imagination is only necessary when we work in the astral or with closed eyes—and for these purposes, simple sigils are quite adequate. When you have created a few scores of sigils you will know which to use in the physical and which in the astral.

Now we want to transmit our sigil shape into the deeper realms of the mind, realms that function with different laws from the surface regions. How do we open the gates to the deep? Austin Spare emphasized the use of vacuity and exhaustion for this purpose. Under certain conditions of consciousness, our armour of habit and self-assurance acquires gaps, cracks and holes through which the unknown may be reached. We have to exhaust or suspend our conscious identity.

There are several strategies for this purpose. Physical exhaustion is very useful. Good practices are: long walks in the wilderness, dancing, chanting, sex, martial arts practice, etc.,—anything that makes you forget your civilized personality, makes you sweat heavily and raises body consciousness.

Identity can also be suspended/exhausted/dissolved through crisis. Disappointment, pain, doubt, morbidity and disease all tend to create holes in the fabric of our personality, to take the meaning out of necessity, and to dissolve the restrictions acquired through stagnant belief. In a sense, crisis may be regarded as a chance to get rid of the useless, and to see the world anew. Thus a period of doubt and trouble may be an excellent occasion to touch the deeper aspects of your being. But however useful crisis may be on occasion, we do not have to evoke it deliberately. Though crisis is one of the most useful tools for dissolving stagnant belief (identity), we need not depend on it. Above all, we should not assume that 'more crisis equals more fresh inspiration'. We do not have to tear ourselves apart in order to produce a gap through which our sigil may pass. Crisis should be neither sought nor avoided—what we need is simple honesty.

For sigil magick we require a gap, a void space through which the sigil may be transmitted without interference from ego. Crisis may produce this gap—but there are many other ways. How much effort do you need to open up, to become empty and void?

There are plenty of misconceptions concerning this matter. The important issue is the strength and persistence of your ego. The person with a big ego will need much greater effort to achieve vacuity than the person who lives at the edge of reality and tries to avoid self-importance and similar traps. Many magicians need great effort—weeks of fasting, holy oaths, special disciplines, long retirements, costly materials, secret formulae, sexual abstinence, formidable invocations, complicated rituals and whatnot—to achieve results that occur almost of their own accord with magicians who take themselves less seriously. Greater effort does not equal greater results. The magician who pretends to divine blessing, deep wisdom, sacred authority and exalted illumination is usually quite incapable of laughing at himself and needs such drastic measures to get his effects.

Ego may also be suspended through joy—intense pleasure, love and exhilaration will easily void the mind and open the gates to the deep.

Drugs are difficult. They may open you up, but unless you are well used to them and have taken just the right amount, they will disturb concentration, thereby distorting the transmission.

Other times when you are 'open' are the 'alpha' phases of half-sleep or light hypnosis—here, sigils may be used that are simple to imagine—or the strange state called the 'Magical Time'. The 'Magical Time' cannot be caused by effort: it arises of its own accord, and in a mode that depends on the individual. It's a state of non-rational functioning, a wide-eyed, open-minded waking dream, during which time seems to stop and consciousness embraces the surroundings with intense lucidity. Modern-day devotees of the ancient Egyptian goddess Maat call this event 'the vortex'; psychologists claim that in it, consciousness is acquired by areas of the brain of which we are not usually aware. All of these states suspend ego and are suitable for sigil magick.

When we have achieved a measure of vacuity, we may transmit the sigil. The basic formula is very simple: empty yourself; make contact with the deep; embrace the sigil; allow it to submerge; close the gap, then forget.

Some magicians seem to mistake the 'opening' phase with the act of transmission. Crisis, exhaustion, intense sexuality etc., all tend to release energy; this energy, they believe, should be charged into the sigil to make it dynamic and strong. It is a common notion, and a mistaken one (let me add that I believed this sort of nonsense for quite some time myself). This method uses dissolution or crisis, whether pleasant or painful, to create a current to fill the sigil with force. Usually it goes hand in hand with the notion that 'more force equals better results'. If the sigil fails to realize, they try to increase the force. This means that more crisis is needed, or heavier ritual, more exhaustion or 'stronger orgasm'—it doesn't matter. The usual result is cramp and frustration (more on this and similar problems in the next chapter). As Spare pointed out: 'There is no need for crucifixion'.

How do we transmit the sigil?

We open our minds and allow the form to fill the whole of our awareness. This is not the sort of concentration that requires force and effort, under proper conditions, awareness settles naturally on the shape, feeds on it, feels it, imbues it with sentience and life. We feel silent and very much aware. We may need effort to open the gates: there should be no effort during transmission. We must be empty to receive. Above all, we should not be concerned with notions of pain or necessity, such as may arise easily during crisis.

Focus all your being on the sigil. Feel it deeply. That is enough. Keep your mind void, your awareness focused on the sigil. Allow your awareness to merge into the lines, to feel the shape, to instil sentience into the seed. Now all kinds of phenomena may appear. The lines may seem to move, the paper may dim or grow radiant, the shape may go 'out of focus', vision may double or whatever. Don't be bothered: keep your awareness gently on the sigil, calm and relaxed, and avoid cramp. The phenomena may indicate that you are touching deeper levels, though this, in itself, is not really important.

It may happen that strong sensations appear. As the sigil is moving into the deep, it may stir all kinds of strange entities or things. There may be strong emotions, or distractions that attempt to lure your attention away. There may be muscle spasms, involuntary motions or urges that annoy. Sigils take curious passages, and may accidentally raise all kinds of waste products from their twilight sleep. Ego may try to interfere, to make you stop, to close the gate. Whatever happens, don't worry. Allow what rises to pass through you and be gone; don't struggle, don't resist; just keep your attention gently on the seed. It may happen that you fall into a deeper trance state: you might lose your sense of time, or find that your body trembles, shakes or sways. None of this is important to your task. Keep your awareness on the sigil and avoid cramp.

It may be that your original desire is vividly remembered. This is especially useless, as it tends to associate the sigil shape with all the fears, desires and anxieties you want to avoid. Don't bother with the desire: care for the form of the sigil, and nothing else. You don't have to tell your inner self what the sigil is for, nor the sigil where to go on its way through the deep: the seed knows where it belongs.

The sensations that arise during transmission should be neither fought nor sought for; nor need you judge whether they are due to disturbance. Spare described the ideal transmission as 'union through absent-mindedness'. Usually the transmission involves several phases of excitement and tranquillity. The excitement—such as swaying, shamanic trembling etc.,—clears the passages and controls the depth of the trance, while the tranquillity gets the message through. Cramp is dangerous as it blocks the transmission, and associates the sigil shape with troublesome emotions.

After a time, you will feel that you've had enough: resume the practice on another occasion. It may be useful, for example, to create the sigil at the new moon and to work with it whenever you feel like it, until the full moon. This is not to say that the working depends on the lunar phases, just that they may be used for confirmation.

After each working, the sigil should be forgotten and ignored. As you will soon find out, the very simplicity of the transmission may be a difficult achievement indeed. A mood of 'friendly indifference' may help. This is what Austin Spare meant with his 'Does not matter—need not be'.

A Ritual Example

1. Exhaustion.

A long journey on foot to a magical place, such as a mountain top, a sacred grove, a lake or some site you feel related to. See to it that you don't think about everyday matters on the way, and that you sweat a lot. Difficult conditions—night, cold, heat, storm, danger, etc.,—may help to upset your ego and open the gates. A mantra is useful.

2. Transmission.

Having arrived, start with a ritual opening and purification. Invoke your gods, spirits, totems (or whatever aspects of self you work with), then go into a trance through dancing, chanting and music. Lay the sigil out: use a simple instrument that you can play while looking at the sigil.

There should be a pattern of alternating music and silence. If you can let go into shamanic trembling, this is quite alright as long as there is no cramp or strain to it; on the whole, it is not essential. Go with the flow; don't resist excitement and don't indulge in it. During the silent phases, allow the sigil to sink in deeply. It is not necessary to desire, or will, or to inflict your ideas and concepts on the seed: experience it fully, that is enough.

3. Release.

After you are done, give the sigil a kiss and bury it. Lay a few flowers on top of the earth and sprinkle some wine on it. Stand or dance nearby, then give your thanks, end the rite and depart.

This is just an example of a ritual framework to suit the actual transmission. You might just as well avoid the 'extroverted' technique—music, chanting, wilderness experience etc.,—and achieve your trance in the 'introverted' way, i.e. deep self hypnosis.

Somewhere between these two poles lies the field of sexual magick. Here we should consider that the union relies on love to transcend ego—if the feeling of love is absent, identity is not transcended and transmission cannot obtain. Love implies that both partners trust each other; this means that you don't burden another with sigils or energies S/he cannot cope with. Crowley's *Rex De Arte Regia* diaries are a good example of how sexual magick should *not* be practised. If you use a prostitute who does not even know what is going on, your supposed 'magical union' is really masturbation, and not even honestly that.

Some magicians advise that a sigil should be worked with until the result manifests. I consider this attitude wrong: the sigil will manifest when conditions are suitable for its growth. If they are not, no amount of stubborn persistence will manifest the desired result; instead, all the futile effort will imbalance the mind and cause frustration and cramp.

There is a variety of sigil working that uses great intensity. This is the case when we work with some god, beast, spirit, or whatever, in a state of direct obsession, as is typical of certain forms of Asiatic Shamanism, African Voodoo or North European Seidr (literally 'to seethe', 'to boil'). Such a session may become a pretty wild affair (depending on the nature of your 'guest'), with plenty of shouting, physical trembling, convulsions etc. In such cases the 'guest' working through your body may take control and directly charge the sigil. This is not the same as when you consciously charge it yourself, as the guest's presence already suspends the interference of ego. Nor is there much need to empty the mind. Vacuity suspends ego—which is not needed in this case—and permits transmission to the deep, which is also unnecessary, as the deep itself has risen to the surface.

Beneath the Surface

The nature of the earth is essential for the development of the seed: seeds grow under conditions proper to them. The conditions under which you live are the ground in which the sigil will flower. A seed planted in the wrong ground cannot develop; it will know that conditions are wrong and suspend activity. The sigil knows which conditions are needed for its manifestation: where will dictates suspension of development, it will wait and rest and dream. The efficiency of the sigil does not depend on the magician's efforts, but on the condition dictated by true will.

Sigils are used where conscious will finds its aims frustrated. We use sigils to bypass adverse conditions, to avoid the censorship of identity, to achieve our will through avenues which we do not even know about. If you think about results while transmitting, you effectively bind your mind to find a solution along the desired channels, and this is frequently a hindrance, as the 'desired channels' are usually the very approach that does not function. Our conscious selves are often the greatest obstacle to the sigil's manifestation.

The active agency of sigil magick is the subconscious self. We need not 'charge' a sigil with our power—the power we can raise consciously is nothing compared to the power that moves under the surface of our conscious mind. The sigil need not be energized—given proper transmission, it will find its way into the deep currents of true will and dynamic instinct, and imbue these with its message. Such a sigil will become irresistible.

Experience will soon reveal that some sigils manifest very swiftly, while others take time and some do not manifest at all. This is determined by your true will and by the conditions under which you live. A sigil that goes against your true will, or that of any other person, will not receive the necessary force and remain latent. Such sigils are considered 'alien material', and expelled by the system as soon as possible. This may happen through confrontation—you will be allowed to learn from your mistakes—through nightmare, crisis, or in the astral, when travelling the darker tunnels of your mind. The dark gods aid the purification of the soul: you will be shown what once you foolishly desired, to digest and recycle the waste material.

In certain cases, the sigil may manifest in an unexpected form. Instead of getting what you hoped for, you may find that the need evaporates, or that the desire is transcended through 'illumination' or changes in your personality. The subconscious self is not a dumb brute that can be ordered around, but an highly intelligent entity.

Then there are sigils that cannot manifest immediately, due to averse conditions or wrong opportunities. Such sigils rest in hibernation and wait for the proper season for their growth: the seed will know when winter is over and life is possible once more.

If many other sigils for the same 'impossible desire' accumulate in suspension, they may seriously imbalance the mind. In some cases they may find some sort of manifestation through wish-phantasms, hallucination or symbolic enactment; in others they may erupt violently or cause the desired change by breaking down the obstacles. In the latter case we do get the desired result by being violently transformed from within.

Sometimes suspended sigils get a chance to incarnate when our habits and beliefs are disrupted, be it through crisis and disease or through changes in our lifestyle. The state of our identity creates the climate and conditions in which the seed may develop: we are the surface of the earth, and as such, select which sigils get a chance to grow.

Consider that a flower needs specific conditions. The ground has to be firm enough to hold the roots, soft enough to allow the plant to grow through; it has to contain nourishment and the waters of life. There should be sunlight, free energy to circulate, and space for the plant to grow and develop.

Some magicians are overly keen on results and try to make the sigil grow by applying intense 'charges' to it. If it fails to grow, they increase the charge, or try to make the gate bigger (more crisis), apply more elaborate formulae of power, or go in for secret rituals and awesome sexual sorceries. Such things may help the desired result if they should happen to remove the obstacles by accident, but usually they don't. The magician has by now become frantic with urge and necessity, and has to fight the fear of failure. Before long he will be so focused on the denied desire that the gates close reflexively, lest the passage be violated.

When we encounter a wall headfirst, do we persist in running against it? Stubborn persistence is often connected with egoistic motivation, i.e., the mistaken belief 'I know my will and I'll make this thing happen'. 'Failure' is recognized as a threat to ego—the same ego that so happily pretends to have divine power and authority—and so the magician cannot help himself: he has to struggle and persist, regardless of the pain. The whole thing is usually considered a 'challenge' or 'ordeal' in such cases—anything rather than accept that one might be wrong.

Seeds should be placed gently. Given the right conditions, a sigil will need fairly little effort: in its own subtle way it will contact the universal will and develop with more grace and power than we can dare to imagine. One of our tasks lies in living the right conditions: it's easy to receive the inspiration for a painting, for example, if you have developed the necessary talents in accordance with your will. If you believe that you can't draw, the sigil's force will have to change your belief first, or make you draw when your inhibitions are low.

Your beliefs are one of the major obstacles to the sigil's functioning. This is why Austin Spare emphasized the use of periodic belief-dissolution—such as the 'death posture'—to dissolve rigid convictions and to give the Self a chance to adapt to new possibilities. To avoid sloppy dissolution ('I'll keep this belief; it's really a truth, but the others may go for good!'), the death posture dissolves all belief that we grow aware of, and allows the personality to reconstruct itself out of a vacuum. If the cherished belief is really a truth, it won't be hurt by dissolution, but reappear inviolate after the cleanup. Regular belief (identity) shredding keeps you sufficiently fluid to accept wilful change easily. This is why Spare depended less on ritual and more on honest living. All in all, a state of what the Taoists call 'Wu Wei', Not-doing or doing without effort is suitable.

Forgetfulness is another important consideration. If you forget your sigil, you won't have to worry about the how and when of its incarnation. Some desires cannot incarnate when one is anxious about results; this is especially the case when the desire involves psychological change. Your ego might try to influence or censor what appears, to speed up the process or control its development. Plants don't grow faster if you pull at them. This is why we forget the sigilized desire after the shape has been drawn: we don't want the ego's influence during transmission or afterwards. Of course it's not easy to forget a desire that seems absolutely vital to you: in this case you may begin to pretend 'indifference', the essential 'does not matter—need not be' attitude. One can learn to forget things: just as it is possible to imagine something, one can also imagine something away—and does so more often than one is aware of.

Begin by pretending that you do not know what the sigil is for. Each time the memory arises, you tell yourself that the memory is probably wrong and certainly unimportant, and that you cannot know for sure. This creates a mood of indifference. Soon enough your play-acting will have caused real forgetfulness.

Sigil magick requires a level of confidence: only in retrospect will you realize that the technique seems to work. What happens to a sigil will only be known when the new thing is there, or when you can look at your past and realize your illusions.

Austin Spare's philosophy of Zos Kia is closely related to Taoism. It cultivates a special open-minded honesty, a sophisticated naivety that feels restricted by certain convictions, and embraces paradox as a matter of course. Life is experienced as something that goes beyond the duality of being/voidness; the same goes for self and anything else. It is a quality that is learned by self-discovery—something that is, and is not, beyond our fumbling attempts at definition; a dance of life and death that finds meaning and balance in the act of going. The sigil crafter never knows for certain, and will always be surprised. Sigils are hindered by absolute beliefs, firm convictions, necessities, habits, conditioned reflexes, routine behaviour and the like—and so are you.

Joy is more important than refined technique—the Deep Ones will care for what is given into their realm; the seed will know the season for its growth.

Lilith

Chapter Three

'Automatic Drawing'

Automatic drawing is not automatic: art is never quite automatic, and neither are you. The term is completely misleading. Usually, the term 'automatic drawing' is meant to designate pictures that seem to appear of their own accord, outfolding naturally with little effort or intent. The technique was made popular by Theosophists, Spiritualists and the Surrealist movement.

A spiritualist medium would fall into some sort of trance and produce drawings under all kinds of absurd conditions. After the session, S/he would pretend that some spiritual agency had used him/her as a vehicle 'because I cannot draw at all!' Frequently people need to insist on the 'automatic' origin of their creations when they dare not assume responsibility for them. It's so much safer to claim 'I can't draw but sometimes the spirit of Leonardo comes over me...', as if that spirit has nothing better to do! I've seen drawings done by 'the souls of great artists', and on the whole, a child could produce better results. It's always easier to blame some spiritual agency than to assume the responsibility of recognizing and developing one's own talents. As if the 'spiritual agency' instils the lines with some special virtue! This is why I dislike the term 'automatic'—it has a taste of self-deception. All true art is 'automatic' insofar as it comes naturally—but this doesn't mean that you have to fall into a fit or suffer a blackout. The 'it came over me and I couldn't help doing it' excuse of the traditional medium simply indicates that the person has so much ego that the dramatic effects are needed to get anything through at all. Such people are often intensely proud, both of their spirits' talents and of their own incapability. Their belief 'I can't draw' is so rigid that extreme measures are needed—measures which are not necessary for Thelemites, who recognize the potential for creativity—Behold! Within and not above!—in all human beings.

It doesn't matter whether we call the source of the drawing 'spirits', 'gods', 'demons', 'inner genius', 'subconscious self' or whatever. As long as we cooperate with it, there will be no need for complete possession and supposedly 'automatic' activity. Above all, we should rid ourselves of the notion that 'automatic' art is something strange, dramatic or mysterious. In its ideal state, the act is simple and natural. The question 'Is this my doing or that of another agency?' is unimportant. What matters is that the picture comes through, that it is vivid and alive.

All art moves between the extremes. On one hand you have the conscious self, which may learn to see and draw through observation and practice. This is the aspect of the artist that gets developed in art school, doing exercises on perspective, landscape, portrait, nudes, etc., with the aim of developing the ability to see, draw and reproduce form. On the other hand there's the subconscious self that expresses itself in dynamic outbursts of total creativity, caring little for convention or control. This aspect of the artist is developed through dreaming, wild living, and breaking through restrictions. In a good work of art, the two aspects balance. The subconscious self supplies the power and the life; the conscious self gives a shape to the whole that makes sense to the observer. The subconscious self, by the way, does not have to be trained, but released. Children are often very good at 'automatic', i.e., spontaneous drawings; they lose this ability once they grow old enough to learn conventions and technique.

When I speak of a 'subconscious self' in this context I do not mean that we are unconscious during the process of drawing. All art is conscious; it's just that the 'I', the notion of identity and control, is sometimes forgotten in the intensity of creation. In this case we forget who we are, and watch ourselves at work. The distinctions between the two sorts of art are fluid; one frequently shifts from one attitude to the other in the process.

Think back to your childhood. 'Automatic drawing' was once natural to you. Watch children of various ages when they draw. If you want to rediscover the talent of inspired art, you will go through the same development once again. Most adults have believed in their own inability to draw for so long that they cannot allow the hand to move freely; thus our task begins with getting rid of these restrictions. Our major problems are effort, deliberation, result-orientation and cramp. Beginners are often afraid of recognizing their ability. Some people have hidden in the belief 'but I can't draw' for so long that they fall into crisis when you prove that they can. Others feel terrified by the strange convulsions that arise out of their unacknowledged identity. The temptation to deny talent and give up the practice can be overwhelming.

Some simple exercises

Get yourself plenty of big pages (at least A3), preferably something tough and cheap: wallpaper and brown packing paper are excellent. It's important that you start in a big size, and have no hesitation in using up great amounts. Use several sorts of pencil. Thick lines, as from a soft pencil, are very good for the start. We want to avoid hesitation or doubt. Thin lines, as from a hard pencil, are useful if you wish to overwork the design with ink. Thin lines can be erased more easily.

Our basic exercises depend on drive and power: 'little pictures', done in frail and indecisive lines, should be avoided. Begin with simple circles and spirals. Cover several sheets with all sorts of circles, continuous lines that rotate swiftly. Try some changes. Watch your hand revolving; get used to the rhythm and flow.

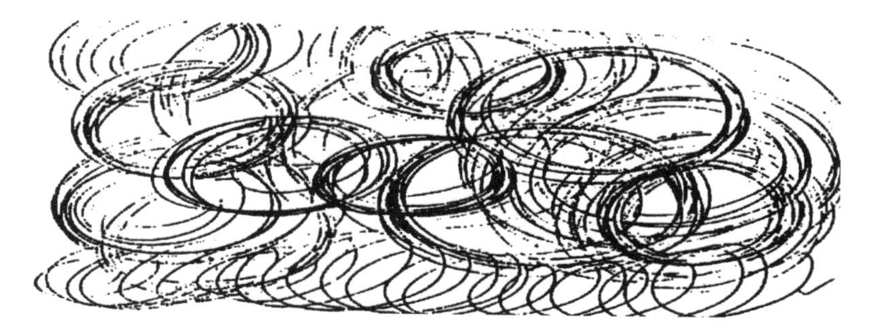

The important thing is the feeling of drive and intensity. Try to change your grip on the pencil and find out what happens. This practice may seem simple, but that is no reason to neglect it. Get well used to the feeling of moving the hand swiftly and with power. You should cover dozens of sheets in this way, even if it may seem boring. Then try with closed eyes. Invent variations. Vary your speed and the pressure on the pencil.

Next, you may try some other shapes that require little thought and plenty of abandon.

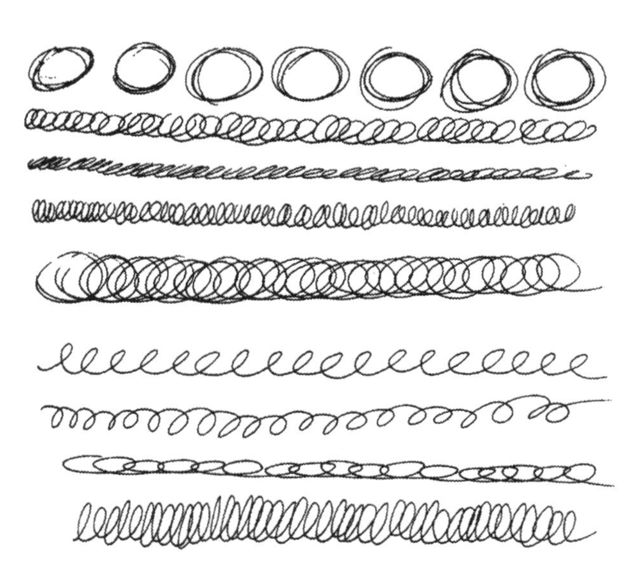

Cover at least two pages with each of them. The pattern itself is not as important as the question of getting used to moving the pen with power and swiftness.

A word on difficulties. Our major problem lies in the beginner's belief that his output is inadequate. This feeling of failure restricts the free movement of the hand. This restriction may cause several symptoms, each of which is obvious from the flow of the pencil. As I can't encourage you during your practice, we will have to begin with the very simple things that are not too frustrating and reveal the problems you have easily.

There are three basic varieties of beginners' troubles, which can be classed under the headings of the alchemical principles.

'Salt' symptoms are slow, coarse lines, a sluggish hand, a tense wrist and stiff, laboured symmetries. Such cases should work on their power and fluid motion.

'Sulphur' troubles show in uneven outbursts of power, usually dictated by temper and emotion. Moments of weakness alternate with sudden explosions; the artist is often in a hurry, lacks patience and tends to break the pencil tip or to rip the paper. Try to keep your temper and to let the power out in a continuous flow.

'Mercury' problems show in uncertainty. Here the line may become thin and wavering, as if the artist almost dare not touch the paper. There is a fear of commitment; the lines look weak and frail, or may break too easily.

There is a dangerous tendency to fall into doubt and to lose the impulse through repairwork. Such cases should not use the eraser at all. Try to keep your work in a big size and move the pencil decisively.

Most beginners have problems. Don't let them bring you down. Also, you should not try to evaluate your output. If you try to learn 'automatic' drawing, you are creating a gate through which the deep may reveal itself. Your ego will possibly dread this possibility, and try to convince you that your efforts are useless, your results lousy and your 'real talents' elsewhere. It may compare your work with that of 'real artists', steadily ignoring the fact that these have had just as many troubles as you have. For this reason I always pretend that the whole thing is 'just a game' when teaching others; it helps to keep the result-orientation under control. Don't take the exercises too seriously.

Here are some patterns that develop rhythm and flow. Observe your speed and timing. Fill at least two pages with each of them, and invent some variations.

The following exercise develops the ability to draw 'units' of linework in a swift and spontaneous manner. It helps to learn about space, flow and interruption.

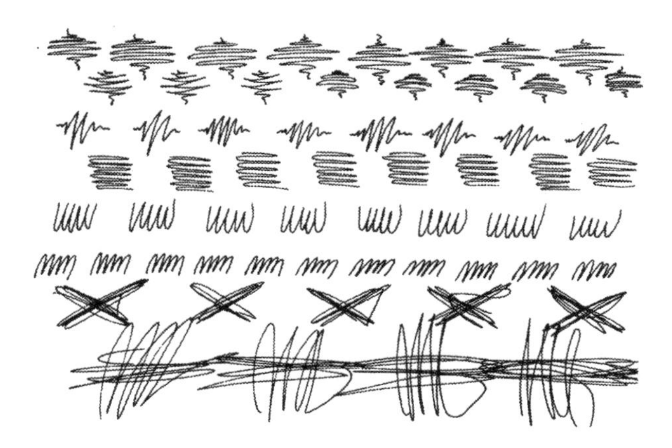

Try different sizes and invent variations. The important issue is the hand's ability to move freely and with power. Some find it helpful to cover pages until they are almost black. This is the hand's way of screaming 'Don't hesitate: Do!'

Next, we want to get rid of the restrictions that school has imposed on our handwriting. Just as the shaman learns to speak and chant in chaos-language, the artist-magician learns to write in chaos-letters. This may be called 'the dancing line'. You simply allow the pen to perform 'meaningless' squiggles at a speed that frees it from conscious control...

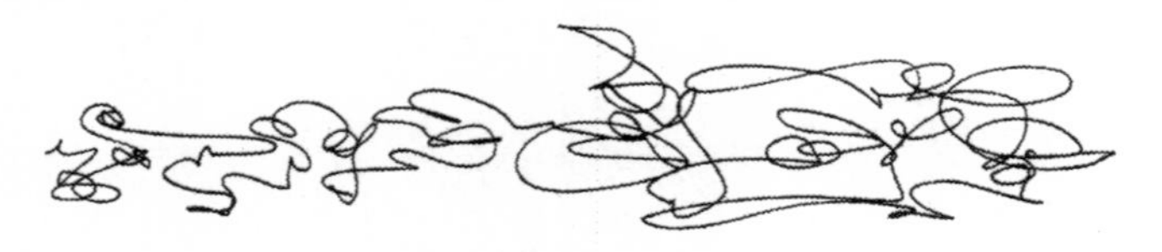

Below is a friendly letter to you, written in chaos language. I suggest you compose several of your own, and mail them off to likely victims.

Impulsiveness is the required quality. If you write like having a fit, you are doing well. This practice helps to get rid of the pressure and control acquired in school. If you try to read the text aloud, it will do the same for your voice. When this exercise has become easy, by the way, you have begun to draw in an 'automatic' fashion.

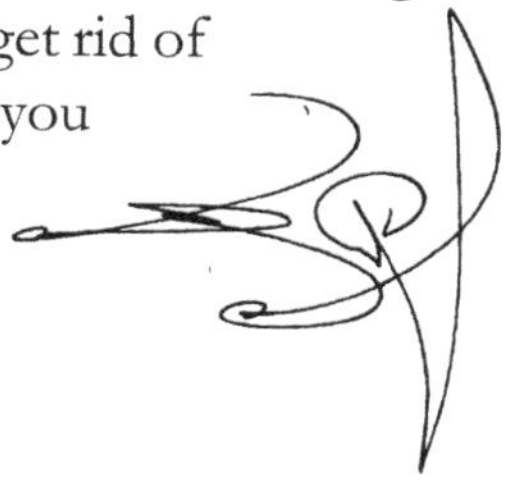

We may now proceed to condense the continuous flow into units, swift outbursts of spontaneous motion. What do we learn in these 'unconscious' spasms? To develop significant shapes 'on the spot', and to stop the action before the structure becomes overly complicated. When you have learned to produce these and similar structures effortlessly, you will also be able to fill pages with such items, be it as separate units or as one continuous interwoven line.

Sigil crafting, according to Frater Custor, will be quite easy to you. You may also experiment with the use of such spontaneous sigils as these—perhaps they may be of use for magick or divination? A well drawn spontaneous sigil can be just as interesting as an *I Ching* hexagram. If you produce plenty of sigils in this fashion, you will soon find out which structures are repeated frequently. These will reflect your major obsessions. You might carefully extract them, simplify the shape, and work with them just as you would with a sigil.

It seems likely that Spare's 'sacred letters' were developed in this fashion. You need not know what each is meant for in order to achieve effects. The structures achieved by such effortless outburst will often suggest meaningful shapes to you. This is due to the mind's tendency to interpret the unknown by means of the known, and to impose order on chaos for reasons of safety. We get the same phenomenon when we look at a gnarled root and determine what might be carved out of it. Vacuity—an empty mind—is helpful to make pictures arise.

You may use the spontaneous sigil as a fundamental structure and develop it, making a picture out of what you have received. This gives you a chance to explore ideas that came originally from your subconscious. It is also good training for your imagination.

It should be noted that 'automatic' drawings are rarely perfect when they emerge. They may reveal their inner essence, but they will also contain waste material, useless lines, or spots where vital lines are missing. When we work with pencil we are free to get rid of useless items and to emphasize important ones after the base structure has 'come through'. The distinction is important. While the picture 'comes through' we should not judge or control or interfere. We may watch our hand as it moves. Usually, our comprehension is just a tiny bit slower than our hand is. In an article on automatic drawing Spare wrote:

> *The hand must be trained to work freely and without control, by practice in making simple forms with a continuous involved line without afterthought, i.e., its intention should just escape consciousness. Drawings should be made by allowing the hand to move freely with the least possible deliberation. In time shapes will be found to evolve, suggesting conceptions, forms and ultimately having personal or individual style.*

Form, Vol 1 No 1, April 1916.

'Automatic' drawing gives your inner self a chance to get rid of repressed materials. This means that some of your drawings will seem terrible, sick, evil or disgusting. It's not important whether you personally like them or not. The thing is there, and should be dealt with. Art gives you a chance to come to terms with it. Don't close your eyes: confront the demons that you've raised. Can you learn to look at them without fear or loathing? People who seek only beauty and harmony restrict themselves more than they know. If you give body to your horrors you may heal yourself. If you deny them, all of your being will suffer. Don't censor yourself. Art need not be beautiful as long as it's alive. Restrict just one aspect of your art, and soon enough the whole of it stagnates.

You may notice that we have dealt with the phenomenon of 'automatic' drawing without reference to the creative agency. We try to learn how to let things happen without care for some specific being that might do the job. It's easier this way. Some more orthodox mediums try to get a special 'person', 'angel', 'spirit' etc., and find their technique cramped by such questions as 'would my guardian spirit draw such things?' In short, they try to limit the scope before they've even begun. Only when you are well used to the practice may you try to evoke one of your 'alternative personalities' (gods, demons, spirits, power-beasts, etc) for the job—but do try to get some experience in shamanic possession first.

Chapter Four

Sigils, Sex & Beyond

Ever since Austin Spare demonstrated the efficiency of his unorthodox methods of sigil crafting, interest in this Nu Aeon mode of sorcery has been growing. Sigils have become a fashion among the wilder fringes of the magical current, and have, together with the formula of sexual magick and drug experience, been thoroughly misapplied by the result-hungry. There are many texts concerning these matters, few of which are worth reading. To the average magician, sigils mean something like an unlimited bank account combined with 'shopping by mail'—results are supposedly guaranteed and all customers satisfied. Nothing could be further from the truth.

Spare's writings, and Grant's presentation of them, have been too cryptic for the mass audience. Numerous individuals and organizations have confused the basic simplicity of the method.

The long desired 'medicine for all ills' should not be sought in the technique of sigil magick, but in the true will, which determines whether a sigil may manifest. It's a strange fact that most authors on sigils tend to ignore the fact that sigils can fail to materialize. In their opinion, failure is something dirty that affronts the mage's power and control, and has to be solved by the use of stronger and more exalted techniques. It's almost like the search for the biggest, best and most lethal weapon that characterizes modern politics—where a single acupuncture needle does not suffice, they try to use an electric drill. This tendency is by no means new.

There are fashions in magick as in everything else; sometimes it's the most elaborate ritual, sometimes the most secret name of power, sometimes costly 'authentic artefacts', exotic drugs or obscure sexual positions. At the time being it seems to be 'Chaos magick', which, as Yog-Sothoth assures me, is just a pretty name for organized nonconformism. Always the urge for more power, better results, less effort, stronger magick, greater satisfaction; never the realization that 'lust of result' is a disease of the ego, and that the oh-so-dreaded failure can be quite wilful on occasion. We don't have to pretend that we are omnipotent to get things done. Isn't it strange that absolute beginners, who need not even believe in sigils, do get good results, while pompous master-magicians, who desperately believe in 'I will: it must be!' continuously have to struggle against the insight that they, too, are subject to error? What is the price of our struggle for success?

I am not writing these words as an innocent bystander. In more than a decade of sigil practice I have made any amount of errors myself, and tried to deal with failure with greater effort and more strain, until cramp came as a matter of course. Cramp, mental and physical, can be a protection-mechanism, to avoid the intrusion of a hostile force or an alien particle associated with unpleasant sensations. It blocks the sigil's passage.

Spare spoke of self-love, yet how much love for self can there be when ego feels that its dominance is threatened? Or that basic needs and desires are not fulfilled? It took me several years to unlearn the misconceptions that had accumulated around my sigil technique. This text was written to get rid of these complications and to reveal sigil magick as the essentially simple and natural thing it is. The same goes for the chapter on so-called 'automatic drawing', which was added as an afterthought. The practices described in it are not exotic, not 'spiritual' or in any way 'exalted'. They have been useful, however, in teaching how to set a pen to paper in a spontaneous and playful mood.

A number of new methods of sigil working have emerged which I will outline briefly.

From Nema came the suggestion to ease earthing by drawing the sigil on the ground, like the vevers of Voodoo, using flour, grains, ashes, chalk or earth colours. You might walk around this shape for a while doing your usual invocation or prayer scenes, and then dance on the sigil until its shape has disappeared. This connects the sigil form with the ground and with your feet, which is a powerful suggestion to manifest the desired will in living flesh, on earth.

Another practice I can heartily recommend is to write a letter to your gods, totems, spirits, or whatever other aspects of your self you are working with. Even the phrase 'Dear Subconscious Self' will work wonders. Now you don't have to define what 'the gods' or 'the subconscious self' is: the deeper aspects of your mind will understand that they are spoken to, and will listen to your call. Usually I write my letters using rune signs or some other magical alphabet which is easy to write but not as easy to read, so that the ego won't interfere in the act of transmission; and include a few sigils in the text to focus specific issues. If you don't have an efficient magical alphabet, I would advise that you do without the varieties given in the medieval grimoires and ask your deep mind to supply something suitable for both of you. Then you simply make your way through the alphabet, imagining or speaking the sound of each letter until you perceive images—simple signs and shapes—that seem to suit the sounds. It may take a few times until you've evolved a complete alphabet, but on the whole, the effort is certainly worth it.

The vital issue, of course, is that your deep mind supplies the proper associations. This is one of the crazier aspects of magick. Many magicians seem to speak in terms of 'I do this and then I control that...', which emphasizes the role of the conscious self. Often we get much better results when we take the trouble of asking the deep mind for help and advice. Ultimately, it is the deep mind which works the magick, and it does so much better if we consult it, instead of expecting it to conform to our conscious desires and attitudes.

The deep mind will know what works for you and will gladly help you in working will; but, as is so easily the case, the conscious mind dreads to 'surrender control' and pretends to know better anyway.

It's easy to ask the deeper aspects of Self, once one has learned the wisdom of actually doing it.

Most magicians—and I was no exception—have a fatal tendency to prefer all sorts of traditional formulae (followed by endless experiments) to the simple act of asking the deep self how to make things work.

Another issue is the question of how one should speak. Traditional mages have a tendency to abase themselves before their deities while simultaneously bossing their spirits around. This sort of thing is pretty infantile. We are dealing with Self. The 'gods', the 'spirits', the 'angels and demons', the 'beast totems', the 'allies' and the 'subconscious mind' are all words meant to describe specific aspects of a single phenomenon, of which the conscious self is but another aspect. In our magick, we are communicating from Self to Self, and this sort of interaction should be done with honesty and joy. When we speak to 'the gods' or 'the spirits' as we would speak to a dear friend or lover, we will get excellent results.

Does this sound too simple? Do you prefer complicated rituals to simple ones, believing that real magick is always difficult and that change requires effort? I suggest that you change this belief.

Magick can be worked quite easily once one learns to re-believe in innocence, simplicity and direct inspiration. Why use a memorized invocation including 'divine names' and 'words of power' when one can get better and livelier results by 'speaking from the heart' plus a dose of freestyle chaos language and chanting?

Some people need hours of heavy ritual—including temple layout, bath, robes, ceremonial equipment, banishings, exorcisms, invocations, dramatic gestures, prayer, sacrifice and whatnot to get into the mood to transmit a sigil. Such games may be amusing for the ritual practice they provide; on the whole they are an effort of the conscious mind to produce a suitable setting for an operation that is mainly under the

Zothyrian Cladokinesis

control of the subconscious mind. Now I have no intention of making you stop such practices (who knows what functions they may fulfil for you?) and I hope that you enjoy them. However, it may be instructive to try out something new, so that you have the choice of getting your effects with or without the theatrical wonder-working business. Try this if you like: simply close your eyes and speak to your deep mind. You might say something like 'Hey! Subconscious mind! I want to ask for your help. I've got this sigil here, for something vital (though I have forgotten what) and I would like to ask you to help me in its transmission. Would you help me?' Now would be the time to be very open to any sort of feedback, as your deep mind will signal whether it likes to, using images, sounds, words or feelings. Should the signal be unclear, you could say 'I can't quite understand this message. Would you make the signal stronger if you wish to cooperate, and weaker if you don't?'

When the response is positive, you could say 'Well, dear, I am going to open my eyes now, and I will look very closely at the sigil shape. The sigil contains a message for you, so would you please let it come through clearly, and allow it to sink deep until it can join with the current of will?' Of course this method, which is as simple as speaking with a friend, requires that you watch out for feedback.

It is not a remedy for all sorts of situations, but there are many occasions when it will be more efficient than the elaborate ritual procedure. It will give your deep mind a chance to tell you if you are working well, or to indicate that the occasion isn't suitable for transmission, which easily reduces the amount of 'hitting your head against a wall' to an acceptable minimum.

In ritual workings, it often seems to be most efficient to combine introverted (vacuity, inner silence) and extroverted (chanting, musick, dance) methods. It's less of a strain to alternate silent concentration with ecstatic outbursts. We don't have to work a sigil for hours, as the deep mind can learn with surprising speed if it feels like it.

Another method of sigil working is offered by sexual magick. This practice has become pretty fashionable over the last years, mainly due to the works of Crowley, Spare and Grant, and so perhaps a few comments may be useful.

Basically the practice works by concentrating strongly on a sigil or a will-image during orgasm. This essentially simple procedure is made somewhat difficult through the cultural conditioning we receive in childhood, a conditioning of such intensity that most magical orders claim to teach the method only to the higher degrees of their hierarchies.

To focus on an abstract shape while making love is an act that connects the will-seed with several very strong instincts, such as the will-to-join and the reproductive instinct. You will probably need good training in concentration and visualization to focus closely on the shape (in your mind's eye), as any other idea that rises into your consciousness will attach itself to the sigil. This may create some difficult associations. Also, you will have to keep up your sexual enthusiasm at the same time, which can be something of an effort.

Then there is the question of the sexual identity. Most of us got a heavy conditioning which taught us that sex is shameful, or at least something not mentioned in public, and that we should hide our lusts and desires behind a mask of politeness and social conformity. Well, if we connect the idea 'shameful but nice' with a sigil shape, the sigil won't get far.

It's sad but true that most civilized people are sexually cramped, both in their attitudes and in their energetic ability to go with the pulse of the 'orgasm reflex'. The attitude may be changed, using trance therapy and similar methods, but intellectual tolerance in itself is not enough to dissolve the 'character armour' that manifests in various chronic muscle cramps all over the body. Theory on this subject can be found in Wilhelm Reich's *The Function of the Orgasm*; while Hatha Yoga, Pranayama Yoga, Chinese Ch'i Kung and frequent dancing (emphasizing hip motion) offer practical help. Such practices are excellent for releasing chronic tension, which in turn allows the sexual energy to circulate and pulse freely.

Last, there is the pitfall of overmuch control. Some esoteric orders are blind enough to advise their followers that during the practice of sexual magick, neither emotion nor love should be felt. Maybe this helps to keep the willed image clear, but then it also takes the meaning out of the act. In my eyes, sexual magick is pathological if it isn't performed as an act of love and sharing among equals who join their being's essence to give life to a mutual will impulse. Of course, to honest lovers any act of lovemaking is magical, the event itself both ritual and sacrament; and such things as sigils may seem unnecessary complications of a greater union.

Personally, I suspect that the great fuss about sexual magick comes from the fact that most European mages and witches enter the world of magick by intellectual speculation plus reading books and discussing them. This approach includes a dangerous tendency to deny and control the body, to concentrate on intellectual mind games and to ignore the joys of dance, exercise, outdoor activity and the like. When, at long last, they are allowed to do something positive with their bodies (i.e. sexual magick) this may produce a jolt of energy which was hitherto unknown to them. Using the wilder forms of shamanic trance obsession you will get similar results—and you won't need to waste a good session of lovemaking by concentrating on some abstract shape.

Last, there is a form of sigil magick that could develop into an interesting field of experiment. Have you ever played 'cat's cradle' with a longish bit of string? This astonishing game—it can be found all over the world—is frequently associated with sorcery practice. Try to play it in a gentle trance state. You don't have to know what these chance-sigils mean to find them effective. Often, deep problems get sorted out when one plays with the string while reflecting on them. This is also useful as a communicative process. If you have communication problems with a friend or loved one, play it together. Not in the regular fashion, which produces the same set of figures, but by making abstract and irregular designs which you can sort out together. This little spider game can be useful when the ordinary channels of communication are blocked. Hopefully you have the brilliant sort of subconscious mind that likes to experiment and to develop new methods of sigil magick. If this is the case, I would be happy to hear about it.

Bird Dancer

Chapter Five
Visualization

Visualization is a simple and natural skill which nevertheless requires a measure of practice. The mages of the old ages were quite aware of this difficulty. They believed that to imagine difficult sights we would have to learn to visualize simple ones first, and prescribed a number of simple images: points, lines, geometric shapes, colour fields etc.—which the novice was to practice with. I have rarely heard anything except curses from people who began by using these methods.

Simple images can be among the worst for our purposes. If we try to hold the image of a circle in our mind, if only for a minute, we will find that the image seems too simple, or too abstract, and our mind will get bored within seconds. Before you know it, the circle has moved, coloured, erased, deformed or squared and slips out of our attention unnoticed. How do we develop visual imagination if even the most simple practices seem futile or frustrating?

We start out more simply yet. If this were a cooking book, we might begin by getting the cauldron or pan ready. In our case we won't need to buy these tools, as we already have all the equipment for the job. All we require are a couple of senses: we are lucky to have several of them (they come free of extra charge in one package with body and reality at the moment of birth.)

We will also need some energy, which will be supplied by enthusiasm, and some patience. Add to this a friendly subconscious mind which does a good job for you by being kind enough to help you in the working.

The subconscious mind will frequently be called 'the deep mind' in these pages, not because of any measurable depth, but to remind you that the sentience we live with is not the horrid creature Sigmund Freud and so many of his followers made a living out of. As your deep mind has supplied you with this book, we may safely assume that it has a real interest in developing your latent powers and talents.

Creative visualization can be one of the skills that allow the mage to contact and communicate with the deep mind. I trust your deep mind—no matter whether you call it your 'gods' 'inner genius' 'ally' 'spirit helper' 'holy guardian angel' 'totem animal' or 'patron demon'—to find meaning in these words, a unique meaning suited to you and your needs, and I am sure that all of you are capable of developing new and original skills, out of the experiences which this volume holds for you.

Waking the senses

> *Thou art that which thou dost prefer. The seer, the instrument of seeing, or the seen.*
>
> *Austin O Spare, The Focus of Life*

One of the keys to magick is the use of the imagination. Imagination is a plastic medium. Giving form to our beliefs, it creates, supports and destroys the realities we believe. Imagination is an activity of the inner senses. What you may ask, are these inner senses?

What we know of the universe is a conglomerate of experience which we have received through the senses. The phenomena we call 'a tree' consists of several sorts of sensual information.

How does it look? What is the motion of the branches? What shades of colour are the bark, the twigs, the leaves? How tall is it? How do the roots coil? How does it fit in the scenery? Questions such as these can be answered with the eyes. Our ears supply different information-flow. Can you hear the motion of the leaves in the wind? What is the sound of a falling acorn? Are there birds in the branches? Feeling gives us more detail. How does the bark feel? How firm is the wood, how elastic a branch, how soft or crisp a leaf? How solid is our tree, how damp, how warm? We learn these answers by feeling them.

Then there is taste and smell. Do you know the taste of fresh green beech leaves? (When they are young they can be used for salads!) How do the berries or fruit taste? Can you remember the lightly bitter aroma of young fir tips? Do you know the scent of spruce resin? The smell of decay in damp, rotten leaves? The fresh dampness of the fir-forest after a gentle rain?

All of the information comes into our mind through the sensory channels. Like a jigsaw puzzle they fit together and create what we believe a tree to be. When you think of a tree (do this now!), just what sort of sensual data comes into your mind? Do you see its shape? Do you feel its wood? Do you hear the foliage? What about smell and taste? Do memories arise?

Which sensory information was well represented, and which sense did you happen to forget? Think—if you like—of the following phenomena. Which senses are active in your mind and which are absent? Do you prefer any sense for recollection? Try to think of the sea * a mountain * a forest * the place where you work * the place you grew up in * your temple * your lover . . . How do your senses represent them?

Now, however detailed your representation may be, it will not be complete. There may be a myriad aspects to a tree which we will never recognize due to the simple lack of sense which might perceive them. The ultra-violet radiation of the sun is invisible to us. Bees can see it very well, and use it to find their way.

A dog may well think in terms of smell. How does the bat represent its surroundings? How do migrating birds, butterflies, salmon or whales find their way? How about our good friend *Palolo Viridis* (a worm from the Pacific ocean) who swarms only once a year, on a very special new moon? Clearly there must exist a couple of senses which we cannot even imagine (though we ought to try).

An immense amount of sensory data comes into our minds all the time, much more information than we can cope with. There are parts of our deep minds which have learned to select. According to a system of priorities, they provide us with a representation of our sensory experience, and this representation is the fantastic dream that most people consider 'reality'.

One of the scientific fables of the last centuries is the belief that people would share a common, 'objective' reality. If we examine the sensory experience of different people we will soon find out that everyone of us lives in a unique reality of her/his own making.

Occasionally, we may perhaps perceive the same original sensory information, but this is as far as our common experience goes. Our personal history differs, as does our nature, our work, our will and our priorities, and consequently each of us will come to a special selection, a representation that suits us.

More so, this process is so natural for us that it works automatically: our deep minds have learned to respond to specific information, and to represent it in special ways.

A good example would be all those people who wander through nature on the weekend, and who fail to notice all the life around them, as it is not important enough for them. An arachnologist will easily spot a dozen spiders where you will only see one: the same trick can be performed by people with arachnophobia, as spiders are really important to them. I suspect that this selective mechanism works by habit.

Our deep minds have learnt which sensory information seems important to the conscious mind and supplies it vividly. It is no coincidence that the average Marxist lives in a horrid world full of class-struggle, oppression, poverty and futile revolutions, or the average magician in a reality full of gestures, signs, omens, power zones and etheric radiation. We teach our deep minds which experiences are important to us and ought to be emphasized.

This world-view very easily becomes habit and is rarely questioned as it seems utterly real and convincing. Before long we may forget that what we experience is not all that can be experienced, that we live in a selection, not in the fullness of all possible realities. When we remember that we select our reality we may remember to select a reality worth living in.

Exercise one

While you are reading these lines your attention was probably closely glued to the words, to your inner voice, and to the inner sights and feelings that were stimulated by the text. Now we will move attention into the outer universe. Make yourself comfortable. Take a few deep breaths. What are you aware of right now? Begin by speaking aloud. Say what you are perceiving with your senses. You might start with touch, for example. This might sound like: well, *I feel the book in my hands and how my fingers are holding the pages. I feel my body resting in the chair, and my legs are crossed. One of my feet touches the floor. . . I feel my belly moving as breath flows. . . and the motions of my mouth...and the sensation of air on my skin. . . and my body is swaying lightly. . .* And so on.

Go into this experience deeply: there is a vast wealth of sensual awareness if only you bother to recognize it. All of these sensations came through the sense of feeling. Now move to another sense and start speaking what you sense. For example: *and as I feel my breath flowing . . . I can hear the words that come out. . . and I hear the voices of children on the street and the chirping of the birds. . . and I hear my breath flowing. . . in and out. . . there's a car passing the house. . . now the fridge is beginning to drone. . . and there's music in another flat. . .* ' And move to the next sense: *I see the sunlight. . . bright spots moving over the walls. . . shining on the pictures. . . and rays of light coming in. . . I see the dust particles dancing. . . and the rich green of the plants. . . as they soak in the light. . . and the brown spots at the edges of the leaf. . . and the curve of its growth. . . and the deep colour of the earth. . . and I see my body. . . my hands are resting. . . and when I look carefully. . . I can see the fine lines on my hands. . . and the little hairs. . . and so on.*

Repeat this practice for a while. I know it may seem primitive, but unless you really try it out, much of what will be offered on the next pages will be lost.

What happened? Most people who try this practice report that much of their attention moved 'outwards', into the world of external sensory perception. This, in itself, may be a useful ability. How many occasions can you remember, how many times when you were so focused on inner troubles, hopes, dreams or whatever that you simply lost contact with the world around you? When you will yourself to move your attention from the inner to the outer world—which can be difficult in times of crisis or depression—this practice can help you to change.

Another advantage is the ability to 'go into' a sense of your choice. When you have spoken and perceived and spoken some more in a sense, you will find that this sense gets amplified, and that you perceive it more intensely. The more attention you give to a sensory channel, the more intense will the experience be. Amplifying all sensory channels at once tends to produce mind expanding experiences. Another vital issue is learning to speak freely, with few inhibitions or attempts to control. This is going to be useful later on.

Have you tried the experiment a few time and in a few varied surroundings? You may have learned which environments you like to experience deeply and which settings should be experienced less intensely.

Exercise one - variations

Now we can experiment with some variations. First you could learn to change your voice.

1. Change the modulation of your voice so it sounds friendly—make it the sort of voice in which you would like to be spoken to. How does this change your experience?

2. Try to speak fast. Speak in a loud and excited voice, and allow yourself to become faster, and more excited, with each sensation you describe. What happens to your experience?

3. Try the 'ceremonial magick' voice. This sounds sonorous and serious, and vibrates the words in a certain droning manner. Try to sound important, as if each of your words would have a world-shaking impact.

4. Speak slowly and become slower yet. Give yourself a lot of time. Speak *very* slowly in a soft and gentle voice, calm and peaceful. . . and if. . . you say. . . only two. . . or three words. . . with each breath. . . you may find. . . that your mind. . . is calmed. . . and awareness. . . gets richer. . . more intense. . . and vivid. . . and you. . . can relax. . . and allow. . . the experience. . . to lead you. . . gently. . . and easily. . . into a pleasant. . . and restful. . . natural. . . trance state. . . and you may. . . enjoy. . . to be slow. . . and calm. . . to give yourself. . . all the time. . . to sense. . . deeply. . . as it pleases. . . all of you. . . and you are free. . . to move. . . as you will. . . from sense. . . to sense. . . from thought. . . to thought. . . and word. . . to word. . . flows gently. . . as you sense. . . the fullness. . . of experience.

5. When you can produce a lot of interesting changes in your awareness using these methods, feel free to change the loud voice into your inner voice. Allow your voice to calm. Let it become a whisper, a gentle, barely audible, running flow. Then continue in your inner voice. What does your inner voice sound like? Is it a friendly voice? Do you like to hear it? A good many people have awful inner voices which nag and complain and criticize most of the time.

Perhaps they would like to listen more closely to their inner voice if that inner voice sounded more friendly. If the inner voice wants to be listened to, it would do well to sound so friendly that the conscious mind likes to listen to it. We can tell our inner voice how we like to hear it, and allow it to become an inner voice which is a pleasure to hear.

Probably the first insight will be that changing the modulation and the speed of your voice can change your awareness. It has done so all of your life, only you were unconscious of it. Speaking in an excited voice is a wonderful way of becoming excited. We can find a use for this when we are tired and feeling apathetic. Think of what the sport's reporters do on radio. Somehow these professional blabbermouths manage to speak so excitedly and fast that the audience imagines (hallucinates) fast and exciting events, and experiences genuine tension, relief, joy, pride etc.

Using the excited and fast voice you can make the sensory experience of a pleasant day in the woods an event as exhilarating as champagne. Using slow and gentle speech, on the other hand, you can soothe yourself and allow yourself to float into a gentle half-sleeping trance. Many trance states involve a movement of awareness inside. If you use this method—and I can't emphasize just how important this practice is—you will find that at some time your eyes will want to close, and that your mouth wants to be calmer, so that your voice becomes a whisper, or continues internally. This is quite all right. Allow it.

Though your mouth may be closed, the inner voice can continue in its slow and calming fashion. Though the eyes may be closed, one can still see with them, and describe the darkness, and the motion of light on the lids.

When the awareness moves from the outer to the inner senses, you are still free to describe what you sense, and to amplify it. There will be inner vision once the eyes close, although you may not believe this is possible. Don't expect too much. What do you imagine inner vision to be? Can you day dream? Can you remember the house you grew up in? Can you imagine what people see who are really good with inner visions? What do you see in your dreams? What is your favourite colour? What will you look like when you have mastered these practices? What colours are the clothes you are wearing? What would you look like in fur and earth colours? Are you really quite sure that you don't see images with your inner eyes?

This talent can be improved.

There are people who find it difficult to become conscious of their inner senses. When they close their eyes they see darkness, and as they continue to use their physical eyes, darkness is all there is. Inner vision is not seen but imagined.

Remember the tree we began with. Think of that tree now. I say 'think', but what does it mean? Your thinking may appear in the form of feelings, or it may be the inner voice, or you may imagine in vision. When I ask you to remember the shape of a branch, you will need an inner picture to do so. We all do plenty of things with our inner senses, and most of us don't recognize this.

When you are asked to remember or imagine what something looks like, you can only do so by using 'inner vision'—and this is so natural for you that you do it without recognizing it. Indeed such inner visions, inner voices or inner feelings can work with such speed that they are too fast for consciousness.

A simple process like 'I see this, get that feeling about it and say to myself so and so' may take less than a second, as we have done this all through our lives, and all the conscious mind recognizes is the final outcome 'well I thought. . . ', with no awareness that this 'thinking' involved a complex operation using representations in several inner senses.

One of the important issues in magick is the fact that people use their inner senses in different ways. Some people have wonderful 'inner hearing'. They can imagine the voices of their friends, or the sound of rain on the window or the screaming of car tyres. And often they have well-modulated inner voices in which they can hold lengthy debates.

Others have developed their 'inner vision'. Can you imagine what you will look like in ten years? What did your parents look like when you were young? Do you know the shape of oak, rowan and birch leaves? What would a violet fir look like, or a pink beech tree? If you can answer such questions well you probably have developed a good visual imagination.

And then there are those who feel deeply. Can you imagine the feeling of a cold shower, the icy blast of water rushing over your skin? Do you know the glow of hot wine, and how it moves through body? Do you know hard and soft feelings, emotions of heaviness, of flow, of outburst and expansion?

Can you imagine what the touch of your lover is like? On close examination, most people realize that they have 'favourite senses' to represent their thoughts. This does not mean that they use only these.

It seems likely that we use all of our senses all of the time, but that the conscious mind likes to specialize and this sort of specialization may be equally advantageous and restrictive. If you came to the recognition that you are 'this type' or 'that type', let me assure you that you are wrong. As a complete human being you can learn to use all of the senses. Each sense offers a wealth of possible experience. If you have some sense which is especially well developed—try developing the others equally well!

Magick requires a good imagination.

If we imagine a god-form, we will probably start out by using a favourite sense or senses. Some people can hear themselves invoking the names of that deity. Others get feelings of awe or wonder, and others will see that deity, complete with appropriate scenery and symbolism. None of these is good enough. If we want to get a really intense contact, we will have to use all of our senses. What we want is vision and sound and feeling in cooperation, we want to feel and see and hear all at once. So that each sensory channel supports the others and we get a representation as real as real can be.

By now, I hope that you have learned that the mode of speaking—such as tempo, modulation, energy, tone, has much to do with how we perceive what we are describing. You will have recognized that a slow, a fast, a friendly, an excited, a dull, a loud, a whispering, or a sexy voice have all sorts of effects on the mind which have very little to do with the actual information that is being communicated.

You may have realized that naming what you perceive is a way of making that experience more intense. This is certainly not a new insight. . . on the unconscious level, this sort of thing is being done by most people most of the time. If you want a good demonstration, ask someone you don't like what s/he felt like the last time s/he was really sick. Keep asking for details and watch how that person goes into the feelings s/he describes.

The more vivid and detailed the account, the better the chances that they will actually relive that awful experience. . . getting good access to all sorts of pains and worries, and amplifying those memories by describing and experiencing them simultaneously.

Oh dear! What a beastly experiment! Is it unethical to ask another what something awful was like—a question which can only be answered in full and gory detail by getting good access to that memory and reliving it? Should we do such things with others? Well, how often have you done this before, to people you really care for, out of some strange notion of 'compassion' and 'human interest'?

Or would you like to learn the opposite? What happens when you ask for a really good account of what it was like when your test person felt happy, healthy, powerful, dynamic, cheerful or even inspired? What happens to people who like to tell of their good times? Can you observe changes in posture, breathing, muscle tones, skin-colour, rhythm, voice or such?

Exercise two

The next experiment may tell you how much you can perceive if you want to. Try this out with a tree or a plant, as these are living beings with complex forms which are mainly unknown to most minds. First you ought to find a good tree. Walk around it, see, listen, feel, taste, smell that tree. How much detail can you perceive? How much of your awareness can be expressed in words? Give yourself a lot of time and keep speaking.

Did you find this practice difficult? Beginners sometimes try to make their description perfect, or precise, or even poetic. And when the words run out, or the phrases get tangled, they begin to worry, and worry about words, which is miles away from the tree experience they began with.

If you are not used to improvising speeches, prayer or hypnotic poetry you will certainly require practice to become fluent. Beginners often lose their rhythm, or forget words, or halt, or pause, or get the wrong phrase, and repetitions are common. All of these are typical and quite natural. Right now, nobody gives a damn for perfection.

Say what you like. There is no right or wrong in these matters—the only vital issue is that you open your mouth and keep talking. If the words make convoluted dancing movements, this is their own affair.

Repetitions are very useful. If you find nothing new to say, say what you said before until something new comes up. Even if you repeat yourself a dozen times you are doing well—it may not be very original, but it will work to intensify what you are speaking.

Pauses can be equally useful. A moment of intense silence may clear the senses for the next sensation. If you are using the slow, hypnotic speech method, you will find repetitions and pauses useful to amplify the trance. In the long run, the practice of free speech will help you to learn that you can trust your deep mind to find the right words.

If you have trance experience or have learned methods of self-hypnosis or meditation you are probably accustomed to glide into trance in a comfortable, relaxed posture. The basic idea being that when the body is at rest, the mind is free to roam the inner worlds. Some of you, particularly the hypnotherapists, the shamans and the adherents of voodoo or chaos magick, will be aware that trance does not require a passive, or relaxed body. Indeed most trances are not induced by conscious effort and traditional technique, but came quite naturally. Most people are in trance dozens of times every day without recognizing the fact.

Perhaps these natural trances are not as intense as that which you experience when you go into a willed trance, but this is really a difference of degree, not of nature.

Do you remember your school days? Or the university? Can you remember what it was like when something really interested you? Some teachers, or topics, had a way of catching your attention, and you were interested, and enthusiastic, and wanted to know more, and yet more, until all of a sudden the bell rang and you found the hour over, much too soon. . .

And what about the other extreme? Some teachers were really awful. . . talking in a dull and weary voice of strange and incomprehensible alien subjects, so that the words seemed empty and faded into a monotonous background drone and you felt bored and annoyed and your attention began to move. . . to others in class . . . to the window. . . to the squiggles and scratches on your table. . . to the cracks in the plaster. . . to the things you intended to do after school. . . to memories of the weekend. . . etc. . . until the bell rang to wake you.

I would call both of these situations trance states. In the former, your attention was so closely fixed to some outside stimulus (the topic you were interested in) that inside awareness (such as: do I like this? What will I do afterwards? Am I hungry) was largely forgotten.

I tend to fall into this sort of trance when painting. For hours I am so obsessed with colour and form and layout and all the rest of it, that I forget to eat, to drink, to rest...and when the painting is done, I suddenly remember my body and feel totally exhausted.

In the other trance, the outside awareness (such as school, teacher, the lesson, etc) became so dull and unattractive that your mind, being fed up, dissociated the items which did not interest it, and associated with the items that offered more interest and pleasure. In our example, the outside world became so uninteresting that attention turned inwards, and this inner experience became so vivid that the outside experience was forgotten.

We may call this 'daydreaming' or 'hallucination', depending on whether we find it natural or pathological. The same sort of everyday trance can be observed whenever people have to do boring or automatic jobs, or when some inner process (such as problem solving or wishful thinking) becomes more important than the awareness of the outside world. People in very deep depression, or people in love tend to notice very little of the world around them. We are reminded of Milton Erickson's definition that trance tends to narrow attention while making it more intense. As long as we sensed and described outside awareness, our attention focused on the outside world, and we perceived it more intensely than we usually do.

When we switch our description and awareness and focus on our inside awareness and inner visions, words, sounds, feelings, in our minds, we will sense these more intensely than usual.

Some schools of psychotherapy ask their patients to 'go inward' and to describe all that is perceived. Usually through this the inner awareness becomes stronger and more intense. Nepalese shamans practice astral projection without the need for a deeply relaxed body resting in a quiet place. These shamans chant and drum themselves into trance. Then they begin to describe how they leave their body and the ritual area, and how they fly with their guardian beasts, over the village, over the river, over the mountain passes to the invisible worlds, the spirit countries, the realm of the dead and the unborn. The journey is described in song, and much of this song is repetitive, the outcome of many journeys. Such on-the-spot accounts of motion and inner experience make the trance perception more intense for the shaman, and allow the other shamans, and the audience, to participate.

There are a lot of people who need peace, quiet and relaxation to think or daydream. We can get the same effects in many ways. Go for a long walk, preferably in the country, where you can be on your own. If you walk for a while, you will find that the regular, rhythmic motion of your body can be just the thing to soothe you into a pleasant half-sleep or trance state.

Step by step your feet find their way, and with a little practice you can coordinate your walking pace with your breath rhythm. As you walk repeat exercise one.

Exercise one - in the wild

Step by step. . . the feet...find their way. . . and the mind. . . is free. . . to move attention. . . to the senses. . . and you feel. . . how your body moves. . . and the ground. . . under your feet. . . as you walk. . . and breathe. . . and speak. . . the words. . . flow easily. . . just one. . . or two. . . with each breath. . . moving freely. . . and you hear. . . your words. . . and the breath. . . as it flows. . . and the sound. . . of distant birds. . . and you see. . . the light. . . and the wide sky. . . and the scenery. . . as you move. . . the country. . . flows by. . . and you describe. . . what you sense. . . as you walk. . . rhythmic and regular. . . in. . . and out. . . breath flows. . . words flow. . . and you sense. . . so much. . . to be seen. . . so many sights. . . so many sounds . . . so many feelings. . . you are. . . and enjoy. . . a good trance. . . and move. . . as you will. . . step by step. . . naturally. . .

If you enjoy practice in a playful mood, it will be easy. If you take it too seriously, it may be a bit difficult. Occasionally people tell me they find it hard to coordinate the rhythm of breath and steps. One way to get used to it is to practise with a mantra. If you pick a suggestive phrase, such as 'step by step I learn to go in trance' you might experiment saying (with mouth or mind) one word for each step you are taking.

This will help you coordinate the acts of speaking and walking. Again, you will notice that speed and modulation make a difference. What happens if you speak fast and in an excited voice? One thing that can easily happen is that you walk faster and faster. This can become one of the active and powerful trance states, one that can be very useful if you want to walk uphill for long periods.

On the other hand, if you allow the words to move slowly, and equally slow the pace of your motion and the speed of your awareness, you will begin to slide into a slow and leisurely trance. Probably you'll want to stop and rest, sooner or later, to close your eyes and to move attention inward. When this desire arises, feel free to fulfil it.

Sigil gate between the worlds

What can you do once you are in trance? I hope you'll have some answers for this one. If you haven't, how about asking your deep mind what you might use the trance for?

How do you receive your answers? Close your eyes and ask for the creative parts of your mind to invent at least ten possible activities which you might enjoy in your trance. The answers don't have to be perfect. They can be good or bad, reasonable, absurd or downright impossible. It doesn't matter. Collect ten, and then ask your deep mind to select one of them, and to reveal which one it is.

The way to be a really creative magician is to give the creative parts of the mind a lot of freedom to cook up possible choices. The creative parts are there to be creative. If they work well, they will invent anything. They are not very good at estimating which choices are effective, and this is where other parts of the mind come in, to judge, estimate, guess and select which choices may be tried. The same method is useful for painting, as the parts which wield the brush are not the same parts that evaluate the outcome. Were the brush to be applied by the parts that evaluate and criticize, the picture would never get started. This is why good art schools expect their beginners to draw without allowing them to use the eraser.

What many people do when asked to invent choices or alternatives, is that they turn inward in a halfhearted way, pounce on the very first choice that comes up, judge, analyse and evaluate it to shreds, and then decide that they can't invent anything useful. Well, if you were the creative part of such a person, you wouldn't want to work under such conditions either. The creative parts work much better when they are allowed a lot of time and opportunity without interference, so that they can invent a really broad range of alternatives. Even the impossible alternatives are valuable—maybe they won't work, but at least they'll make good jokes.

Coming out of trance is much like reversing the entrance-procedure. If you tell yourself that you will wake up now, make your inner voice lively and excited, take a few deep breaths, stretch, and then open your eyes, you'll be fine. For those who enjoyed the practices and wish to learn more about the sensual channels, the word patterns of hypnosis and many other joys, I would like to recommend the books of Richard Bandler, John Grinder, and Milton H Erickson.

Chapter Six
Access to Imagination

Our imagination tends to take on the forms which we know from the outside world. I might say 'think of the ocean', and what you'll make out of it will have a form, be it in sight, sound, feeling or whatever. In magick, people are supposed to imagine a lot of things. Colours and lights are visualized, we imagine and project signs and symbols, receive inner messages, dream of communicating with such entities as the gods, ghosts, elves or ancient ones and sometimes we create entire dream worlds to explore by travelling through them in various trance states.

Often enough we have to imagine energies, emotions, entities, astral doorways, signs of power or whatever, simply to get the vision and the magick started, and this achievement is not a little one. According to our individual disposition we get along with some of these imagined topics and have trouble with others.

As you will know by now, we are more or less specialized to think certain things in specific sensory forms, so that a painter will easily imagine visual information while the musician may find this sounds difficult. While working magick, we want our imagination to be as real and convincing as we can make it. Perhaps 'reality' has to sound right, or look clear, or feel right to convince you. We may assume that it gets more 'real' the more senses are involved in the experience.

Obviously this means that we have to develop the senses in which we have difficulties imagining. In some cases we will even have to discover them, as with the people who say 'but I never think in pictures' because they are not aware of it.

Last year one of my friends encountered this problem. 'I can't visualize anything' she said, and on closer examination we found that she really couldn't, not even simple objects recommended by tradition, such as blue pigs having samadhi at the seashore. (See Crowley, *Book IV on Yoga*).

I did know something which she didn't. Beginning with the assumption that all people who have all senses also use all senses internally to think. Thus, the visual sense was assumed to be active and lively, no matter whether the conscious mind would recognize it.

Acting on this hypothesis is easy, as it implies that all we need is already there. The huge problem of having to produce an entirely new sense transformed into the much easier task of getting conscious access to a sense which already exists. When I asked her to 'imagine a tree' this didn't work. She tried to construct a picture and found she couldn't, leading to a sense of failure and inability.

Yet when I asked questions that required visual recall, such as 'what does a certain plant look like? Where is object X in your home? How would you drive to get to work?' The answers proved that somewhere in the deep mind, visual information was stored and recalled as desired. The only problem lay in making her aware of it.

I asked her to close her eyes. Then I began to speak slowly, giving plenty of time.

Now. . . I would like. . . to ask you. . . to imagine. . . the feeling. . . you have. . . when your hands. . . move and touch. . . the bark of some tree. . . and you feel. . . the hands moving. . . the firmness of the wood. . . your skin on the tree. . . such a special. . . and strong sensation. . . as your hands. . . move and explore. . . all over. . . the surface. . . the bark. . . the firm. . . solid wood. . . standing before you. . . a true tree. . . with deep roots. . . reaching. . . so very deep. . . into the soil. . . the rich earth. . . so very deep and above. . . there are branches. . . moving.

. . and foliage. . . whispering. . . and perhaps. . . you can hear. . . the sound of the wind. . . in the branches. . . in the leaves. . . moving and whispering. . . and maybe. . . there are birds calling. . . you can hear. . . and feel. . . the wind. . . moving the tree. . . gently. . . and as you sense. . . this tree before you. . . the whole tree. . . you may realize. . . that already. . . you have begun. . . to visualize. . . to see the tree. . . with your mind's eye. . . '

Welcome to vision!

Do you recognize the pattern? We knew that consciously perceived visual imagination did not function on its own. So we began by using another sensory channel, and imagined feeling. When 'feeling a tree' was well established, as I could tell from the little signs, such as small motions of the hands, breathing, muscle tone and posture, we went into the sense of hearing. By the time the acoustic sense was included, the missing sense of vision had come on its own accord. This happened naturally and long before I mentioned it.

Some of you may claim that this sort of visualization is induced by hypnotic suggestion, which is a very dirty word to a lot of people who do not understand it. Of course I used 'hypnosis', as do all people who tell stories, describe events, write letters or books or poetry. Did you sense or imagine a tree while you read the induction? Of course you did, however vague; you had to imagine (or hallucinate) a tree to make sense out of my words. Are you aware that 'reading a book' can be a trance state? What do you do when you read? Body does very little. You move your eyes a little bit, the same regular, monotonous sweep, following line after line of the same dull symbols. From time to time the hand moves a page. You may go on for hours without being aware of it. Reading would be terribly dull, if it were not for the hallucinations that make the words come alive. Words, such as you read or hear, are empty. You have to imagine what they may mean for you and me to make sense of them at all. By imagining this you make them come alive. Indeed, they may come alive so vividly that you'll spend hours devouring a book, completely oblivious of the fact that your body is doing so very little or feels hungry or sleepy. . . and if this isn't a trance state, I don't know what is. Whenever you tell some story, your audience is obliged to hallucinate what you are saying. They cannot experience just what you do, and so they will make sense out of your words by imagining their meaning into them. If you speak well, your audience will be moved by the account, even if all their experience is of their own making.

If you are one of the people who really want to improve their imagination try the method we used to evoke the tree vision. Which sensual experience can you imagine best? If you imagine a stream, for instance, can you hear the water? Can you feel its coldness, the tug of the current, the fresh, damp air? Can you taste the water? Can you smell the decay of the plants at the edge? Can you see the waves rushing, the sparkle of the foam? Some of these experiences will be easy to imagine. Go into them—you can amplify them by describing them—and build up a complete representation.

If you practise this sort of thing for a while, it will become easy. A little more persistence and it will seem natural, and soon enough you'll do it automatically. This means that your deep mind will have learned the process, leaving your conscious mind free to learn something new.

Some complain that whilst they do see with their imagination, the vision seems pale, or shallow, or diffuse. A good example comes from the art of astral projection. In astral projection we are travelling in an imagined body (human or alien) through an imagined reality, a dream world which is created and maintained by the deep mind. In a sense we may say that the astral traveller is journeying through the deep mind itself. Usually the process begins by building up an imagined vision of a doorway, an entrance or a gate. This doorway is imagined in great detail. We imagine what it looks and feels like, and spend a lot of time making it real. Theoretically the next step is easy. We imagine that we are standing before it. We open the door, and walk into the world behind it. What is the setting of the door?

The doorframe connects with something and so does the ground. If we give ourselves time, we can discover an entire reality, developed out of some very small details. Also, imaginary worlds tend to become more real when we begin to explore them. Moving through them leisurely is a good way of attuning to the parts of the deep mind which they represent. Another good access route to imagination is memory. A lot of people who cannot construct images may easily recall them. Let's say that you want to imagine some symbol or sigil, radiant and bright, drawn with the wand in lines of fire. One way to get used to the symbol is to draw or paint it on a large piece of paper, so it may be studied for as long as you like. If you want to imagine this symbol, you need not construct the image in your mind as you can remember what it's like. This technique is sometimes used for god-forms. A god-form is an image of a god we would like to contact. Traditionally, you begin by studying the god of your choice, by reading all legends and myths you can lay your hands on, by painting pictures of that deity, by finding out what aspects of nature that deity represents and what energies and consciousness states it is linked with.

Using our magical pictures, we begin to pour awareness in the right direction. We meditate on the form, colours, posture, attributes, be it by staring at the picture with an empty mind or by speaking, calling, invocation or making music. All of these release emotional energy, which is concentrated and collected by the picture.

Next, we move from the manifest picture to the image we have in our minds. We can remember what our picture looks like. It doesn't matter whether you can paint—do it anyway. To paint the image of a god you will have to look very closely at all the images which tradition has produced, and this is excellent practice as it ensures that you will really see the form, no matter how strange your picture of it may turn out. When you know the appearance of your god, you can build up a very solid representation in your imagination.

Using prayer or invocation, you can call to your deity, and when you are attuned to its nature, you may find that the current begins to flow, the image comes to life, as you have provided the desired

Access to a tree

sentience with a body to manifest in. When you get used to it, feel free to merge with this god, to assume its form and to allow it to indwell, inspire and obsess you. You will realize that the picture which you painted, however good or bad it may be becomes the link between a traditional form and an imagined one. This picture is certainly not the god in itself, but using it as a connection, we may allow the divine sentience to get in touch with us.

This might be said about all anthropomorphic images of the gods. A fire-god such as Loki may be essentially flame, but then we all know that it's pretty hard communicating with a fire. If we want to communicate with Loki, and to unite with her/him, we will find this much easier in an anthropomorphic form. You will understand that fire is a force of nature. The human form, as we make and perceive it, is a convenience to make identification and union easier. We should remember that this is a mask.

If you intend to work with god forms invoke several of them. Monotheism tends to produce very unbalanced magicians. Each god we contact will be linked to another, hitherto subconscious, aspect of our being.

Another interesting point is that you have to be congruent with the god you invoke. If you want to develop the aggressive side of your character, invoke a martial god, such as Horus, Mars, Ares, Tiu, Nergal or Tezcatlipoca (The Aztec warrior deity and murderer of Quetzalcoatl), and do it with power, passion and wildness, as martial deities do not respond to mages who kneel, bow, plead, apologize and try to abase themselves. We have to be like the gods whom we wish to discover in ourselves. If you have become sufficiently aggressive to be real to Mars, you may be sure that the part of yourself which you have made contact with, will show you a lot of ways of being even more aggressive, and in a healthier way.

What have the astral doorways and the god forms in common?

In both cases, our conscious mind created an image and devoted a lot of time and effort to make it as detailed, solid and convincing as we could. About a decade ago, I began to contact my first god-form, Anubis the jackal, who travels the gates and passages and carries the deceased to the otherworld. First I painted a stele, showing Anpu in the traditional Egyptian style, seated, and in profile. Then followed a time of invocation and ceremony, to charge the painting with a lot of passion and power, the energy to get the magick going.

Work with the imagination followed. Whenever I had a spare moment I would recall the picture on the stele and imagine it as clear and vivid as I could. It's easy to make an imagined picture more attractive than a manifest one. We can increase the size, make it come closer, add luminous colours, etc. What do you require in a really attractive vision? Would you enjoy sharp contrast, radiance, sparkle or a soft glow? Does your perception change when you vary the point of view and see the image from below, sideways or above? Add to this a feeling of wonder and inner voice singing and chanting the names of the god. Soon the image will be pulsing with vitality.

One day as I was riding a train it happened. The image had become very vivid in my mind, and as I was in a train, not in a temple, we may assume that I felt very little 'lust of result'. Suddenly the other side took over. Anubis of the desert waste turned his dark head and stared at me with eyes aflame with frozen sothis fire. A shudder shook my body and I found sweat breaking out. Imagination had come alive.

In astral projection, god-forms, beast-forms, tree-forms, shape changing, spell-crafting and several sorts of divination, we begin by creating an image. When we work well, and fill this image with the right energy and sentience, the image becomes a message which touches something deep and powerful within. Energy supplies for this stage are invocation, prayer, deep longing, religious belief, a mantra, song, chanting, sex, dance, offerings of our energy, of body secretions, or the sacrifices of flowers, food or blood. Then the relevant parts of our deep mind will wake and make the image come to life. Sometimes we do well to remember that our conscious minds are quite incapable of predicting what deep mind activity is like. There is a great difference between what we imagine with our conscious minds, and what the deep mind can do, using such an image as a communication channel.

Some people believe that 'the gods' are more than just imagination. If you see the gods as beings outside and independent of yourself, you are right, as they are certainly outside and independent of your ego. If you see them as abstract or natural forces you are right, too, as all the human forms we invent for them are conventions. A solar god, for example, is solar in energy and sentience. To call a solar deity 'male' or 'female' reflects nothing but our cultural beliefs about the way women and men are supposed to behave. Then again, there are those who argue that we are all which we are aware of, and who claim that the gods are expressions of various parts of our deep minds, which are usually not recognized by the ego. This is hardly surprising, as ego recognizes so very little. When the gods manifest, they do so through our senses, through our minds, through our nervous system, and this implies that what we perceive of them is processed through our own system. We cannot tell whether the gods are parts of this system or whether they contact us through it, and for practical purposes this question can be answered as it suits you.

Ultimately all self connects with all self, and thus we do well to consider the 'gods', 'ghosts', 'spirits', 'demons', 'angels', 'totems' or whatever as convenient forms to communicate with aspects of ourselves, all-self, no matter what they 'really' are. Of course we should be careful not to accept any bit of wishful thinking as a genuine manifestation of some spiritual entity. Spirits can and should be tested, as Crowley pointed out repeatedly. If you want to know whether some god or beast spirit is genuine (i.e. inspired by force and consciousness beyond ego) observe how your ego reacts to it. If it gets bloated by pride, delusions of grandeur or the usual tepid 'cosmic wisdom', you can be pretty sure that the 'being' you perceive is a product of your wishful thinking. However, if you find your imagination transforming unpredictably and if your ego feels uneasy or upset you are doing well: the unease of your conscious identity is a good sign that the 'being' you evoked is considerably more powerful than the ego is. Real gods or beasts or spirits can transform the ego, this is part of their job and our magick, and of course ego will feel somewhat queasy about it. Another good sign is that you learn something new and useful, and that you discover aspects of yourself which were previously unknown or problematic. There can be no objective proof, but at least you can be sure that something good is happening.

When we deal with the visions we construct consciously, we are still in fairly safe waters, but when the deep mind out-folds into awareness releasing all sorts of materials ranging from sheer inspiration to suppressed and long forgotten horrors, you may need a good method to cope with the upheaval.

The mages of antiquity were quite aware of this problem. Instead of healing and integrating the painful material, they were quick to call it 'demonic'. Thus they created a model of reality which includes 'good' and 'bad' forces fighting for control, with the 'stupid' ego as sole judge between them. Nowadays, magicians are beginning to find out that the release of dangerous visions has a very good intent behind it, and that even the worst 'demon' of the deep is trying to do its best for the system as a whole. When the deep mind releases some horrid visions, it does so that you may learn to come to terms with them. We can learn methods of dealing with dangerous material without being completely overwhelmed by it.

In ritual magick, there is a practice called 'banishing' that allows us to get rid of or control dangerous material, and another practice called 'invocation' that allows us to contact the sort of material which we want. The two are closely related. In ritual, we begin by banishing our everyday troubles and all thoughts that might interrupt or disturb our ritual trance. Then we proceed by invoking all the forces and sentiences. In astral projection, we banish our awareness of our body and the world around. Then we invoke the dream world of our choice. With god-forms and the like we banish our human identity. Then we invoke the divine sentience to indwell us for the working, and to change and heal our identity from within.

The same mechanism of banishing and invocation can be used to make our visions easier to handle. What we need are some pleasant and some unpleasant memories to experiment with. Students of Neuro-Linguistic-Programming (NLP) may be familiar with the following exercise.

Exercise two - banishing and invocation

When we see a given vision (this may be constructed or remembered) we have basically two choices. One way of perceiving the scene is to go into it, and to experience it as if it happened to you right now. In this sort of vision you look out of your own eyes, feel with your body, hear with your ears, you are fully involved in the event. In NLP this perspective is called 'associated awareness', as you are fully within the scene. The other choice is called 'dissociated' or 'dis-associated awareness', which means that you are not a part of it. Dissociated perception happens when you perceive a scene as if you were outside of it, watching the event, and yourself in it, from any other point of view. If you remember an event from this or from some supposed other life, you can re-live it as if it happened to you now, or you can see yourself acting in the scene, and this subtle difference may have more effects on your experience than you may be aware of.

Some may argue that associated perception is more 'real' than dissociated perception, as you obviously didn't experience the original situation standing outside of yourself. This is a very dubious argument. Memories are constructs. No matter which, perspective can be changed to make memory and vision easier to recall, as suits the data we work with.

Choose a *moderately* unpleasant memory. Nothing traumatic to begin with, just some scene in which you felt unhappy. You don't really want to remember it? That's an excellent sign. You've found the right material to play with. Examine this memory. The contents are not half as important as the way in which you recall it. How do you remember it? Are you inside of the scene, or do you watch it from outside? Try to go into it. Associate with the scene, re-live it as if it is happening to you right now.

When you have recovered—repeat the practice. This time, try the scene with some dissociation. Imagine you are sitting somewhere in the back row of a cinema. The light dims and the curtain opens. Now the memory is shown on the screen. As you sit in your chair you can observe yourself acting on the screen. How does it feel? Can you tell the difference? If you find it easier to cope with, you are doing fine. You can make it easier, by making the screen more remote, or smaller, by making the colours pale, by turning the movie black and white, by changing its speed or by adding another soundtrack. Experiment until you find that you can recall the entire event without being upset.

Feel free to experiment. Now try the same mechanism with some happy memory. Select a pleasant event. Start with dissociation. See yourself acting in the scene. How does it feel? Then repeat the same scene in full association. The scene is happening to you now. What do you feel, see and hear? What is the difference?

When you have experimented for a while you will recognize that the difference is an important one. A typical result of dissociated perception is that it makes dangerous memories much easier to recall and live with. 'When I remember a crisis in associated awareness, the pain and horror overwhelms me, just as it did then, and I am lost in it. When I remember it in the dissociated way I find it easier, as I know that it is past and that I'm not that person anymore.'

This, in itself, is a very useful ability. With good memories, the opposite applies. Seeing oneself in the act of making love can seem absurd or strange. We may get a feeling about the act, but we won't feel what we felt then. It's quite different when we remember the event in full association. Can you go into the memory, feel as you felt, see as you saw, hear as you heard, taste and smell what the event was like? This way you will get full access to all the joy and lust and passion, making recall almost as pleasant as the event.

Some people use this pattern automatically. With my first drastic past-life memories, my deep mind used to change the vision and my point of view whenever things got too tough for me. Others automatically misapply the pattern. There are people who remember the good times in dissociation, which produces vague and unconvincing memories, while associating fully with memories of pain and horror. In their world, the good memories do not count, and the bad ones are the substance of reality. As Richard Bandler demonstrated, we can learn to associate with the pleasant visions, and to dissociate the horrid stuff. This does not mean repressing those experiences. Even awful memories are valuable. To dissociate them means that we dissociate the bad feelings that came with them. We want to keep their information ready for use which is much easier when we are not overwhelmed by them. If you bother to replay a dozen different memories, using associated and dissociated perception as you will, your deep mind will have learned the pattern and will habitually apply it. You will automatically remember the scenes as you willed them to be.

When we experience events which upset us, it is wise to dissociate them from the start. Sometimes it's good to step beside oneself, and to have a good laugh about the situation. When someone is nasty to you, you may cope by playing the usual roles, i.e. defence, counterattack or trying to remain aloof and superior. You might also make the event a chance for something new. When you pretend that you are somebody else, the assault won't hurt so much—and you may find yourself responding in new ways. What would the scene be like if you weren't yourself but, say, a visiting ethnologist, a mad genius, an evil fiend or a court jester? Can you imagine your aggressor in a clown outfit? Can you do it during the event? We don't have to wait until an event becomes memory to change our experience of it. What sort of memory will this moment yield? Is it a moment worth living, a memory worth remembering? How will this moment change when you think of the memory it will make, and change it? Can you imagine what you will

Loki, Fire God

remember of this moment in ten years... and what do you think about it now?

Last year I was exploring the simple art of decision making. One afternoon I came to a crossroads in the woods. I had two basic choices. One was to go on the same level, walking to the meadows, the other was to go uphill directly and to come to the mountain-top sanctuary. Before I knew it, I had decided for the meadows, which is a bit unusual for me. So I stopped and went back in my mind. How did my deep mind represent the two choices to me? Each choice had been represented by an inner vision, with some inner speech, and the feeling this produced was the signal that made the decision. As the process had been so fast, I had hardly seen that vision clearly, and so I went back to examine the representations with more leisure.

The 'journey up the mountain' was a picture of the mountain, all veiled in mist and gloom, seen from very far above so that the trees looked all alike. I was a tiny moving spot moving in the murk, seen from far away. The road of this microscopic figure was undefined, a steep path through uniform trees, a hopeless journey lacking beginning or end.

The 'walk to the meadows' was represented in great detail. I imagined what I would sense there. The rich green of the leaves, wisps of mist floating between the trees, the feeling of damp grass, dewdrops sparkling on tree-fungi, fingers touching moist bark, spider webs between the yarrow flowers. Being fully inside the vision I enjoyed a wealth of detail and wonder. I had made my decision by evaluating two visual representations of the choices I had. As the process was so fast, I was quite unaware of the differences in the representation, believing I had merely 'thought of the mountain and the meadow' and 'had a feeling I would enjoy the meadows much more'.

It's hardly surprising that a vivid and detailed associated vision of joy and beauty raises better feelings than a diffuse and gloomy view showing a tiny fool struggling uphill without goal. My conscious mind believed it had chosen, but the choices had been prepared, to make one much more attractive than the other. My deep mind had made the decision, and as I felt rather weak and lazy that day, the choice was a good one.

When you make your next decision, no matter how minor it may seem, examine how you represent your choices. Are you sure you haven't made the decision long ago?

Here is one of the ways young lovers fall into rapture. All through the day, they dream up wonderful visions, seeing themselves with their beloved. Make your vision large, vivid, detailed, colourful, close. And soon it will seem considerably more attractive than the world around. The trick lies in making a wonderful daydream, often in dissociated perception, and to go into it (associated perception) to get full access to all the good feelings. This releases a strong feeling of happiness, which stimulates us to dream more, and even better visions. In this process, the young lovers will soon be so enchanted with each other that they might as well live in the clouds.

Being unhappily in love can be quite similar. One possibility is that the dreams of fulfilment are dreamed, just as they are in a good affair, but the dreamer does not dare to go into them. A wonderful vision is created, but as the love-sick-one doesn't associate with it, the pleasure is not felt and the result is sadness.

How do you react when you read 'here is a new experiment'? Do you imagine a new experiment as something interesting and pleasant, or do you make it a dull and gloomy vision, and then decide that the 'experiment looks pointless?' How does your inner voice sound when you name alternatives? Can you propose something dull in a voice that really sounds fascinating, or say something wonderful so it sounds quite boring?

There are depressive people who do just what enthusiastic people do, only the other way around. They start out by considering some new idea. This means that they represent the idea in the imagination, as the idea will require a form for evaluation. Now they construct a really awful vision showing themselves in the act of not enjoying it, or being miserable, or suffering. When they have a convincing representation of all that may go wrong and hurt them, they go into the vision and get wonderful access to all the horrid feelings, and then they feel so awful that they won't accept the new idea anyway.

One of the reasons why depressive people find it so hard to do something for their own good is that they cannot imagine anything which would do them good. In such cases when all thinking is negative, the best choice may be to do something, no matter what. Of course the process is very fast. We've been living with our brains for years and years, and find certain things so easy to think that we hardly realize we are thinking them at all.

We can use a similar process to change our minds. Begin by imagining yourself as x (For x fill in anything you would like to be!) Make the picture big, bright and attractive. Bring it closer to you. Go into it. What do you feel like being x? Now make the next picture of yourself, being even more x. Repeat the process until you are satisfied. For those who find this formula too abstract, here is the same process as I received it during a dream.

My dream of being x

Sometimes I catch myself wallowing in dull, morbid or counterproductive thinking and the thought-mill refuses to stop.

1. I recognize that I want to change my mind, as further brooding won't help.

2. I stop doing whatever I did while I was brooding—in this example we will assume that I was walking. I stop and observe. This space is point A.

3. First I observe my inner state of mind. What am I thinking? How do I feel? What do I see within? What does the inner voice sound like? What is my state of mind? How is my muscle-tone? What is my posture? How do I breathe? In this stage, I associate with my inner experience.

4. Next, attention moves outwards. I associate with outside experience. Just where am I? What is the scenery like? How is the weather? Without moving from the spot I build up a good representation of the world that surrounds me.

5. First the inner world was sensed. Then the outer world was sensed. Now I spin around on the spot and leap backwards.

6. Standing at the new spot (point B) I can look forward to point A where I stood a moment ago. Now I imagine that I can see myself standing there, just like I looked a moment ago. No doubt that this figure doesn't look too well.

7. I begin to change this (dissociated) vision of myself. I see myself standing at point A, and improve the vision. I may imagine that posture improves, that breathing flows better, that my muscles relax. And so I build up a vision of what I would look like if I were much happier. Sometimes I change the facial expression of this image of myself and sometimes I add an aura in some radiant colour. When I want to walk into a world of magick I surround the vision with the images of the ghosts, gods and spirits. I make it a good vision, clear, vivid and very attractive.

8. When it is well established, I take a deep breath, spin around and leap forward to Point A, and into the vision.

9. Becoming that vision I get good access to the new state of mind. I start walking fast, and into the new world.

Once you leap into the vision, or embrace it, you should sense a strong change of your awareness. Don't analyse it—to analyse something is to dissociate from it—but enjoy it for a while, before deciding whether you would need another mutational leap.

An Approach To Colour

Colours will be mentioned only briefly because there are so many of them. There are many theories which try to link colours to states of consciousness. Gypsies supposedly paint the sleeping corner of their wagons in dark purple, which is said to make sleep more restful. Theatre dressing rooms are often painted light green, which is meant to soothe the nerves of actors. Exponents of martial arts use a trance in which they imagine a room or space in deep red. Inside this space they see themselves practising or fighting. When the vision is clear and defined, they associate and experience themselves in action, leaping, clawing and kicking in a cloud of rich red light. The red space represents the mood of the exercise, and the mood they may be in when they really need their skills.

I once read of a 'sobering up' cell, which was being tested in American jails. The cell was painted in some awful shade of pink, and was said to sober—or stun—violent drunks within minutes.

In magick, colour is important. Often enough, when we want to imagine abstract energies this is done by visualizing fields, spaces, currents or rays of coloured light. One of the classical techniques of banishing makes use of a field of light. This is radiated in all directions till all negative influences have fled or retired to a safer distance. Giving light a colour may change its meaning. When you paint rooms, symbols, stelae, sigils, or such for your magick, you will probably want to use colours that are congruent with the forces and awareness states that you will to invoke. The usual way of selecting the right colours seems to be the intellectual approach. The word-bound mage plunges into a heap of magical and psychological literature, and finally decides to use a traditional list of correspondences which is supposed to satisfy all. This is one instance in which the conscious mind tries to think up what something may mean to the deep mind. If you are very lucky you may almost be right.

Of course there are some colours that have similar meanings to most people. As long as we work and live by day, light will have a different meaning to dark. The connection of red with blood, or white with age is a very common one.

On the other hand, there are differences. People have favourite colours, for instance, some enjoy red, some thrive on green and others get a real kick from tartan. Some of these differences come from personal history. If you are afraid of drowning, the deep green-blue of the ocean probably won't relax you much. Then there are differences in intensity. Some find it beneficial to surround themselves with a sphere of clear white light. Can you imagine this? What does it feel like? Make the white brighter. Is there a threshold, a point beyond which the image becomes unpleasant? Can you imagine a colour which feels pleasant, and then increase its intensity until it overwhelms? Or try the opposite. Imagine a bright light or colour around yourself and then turn it dim. What happens to your awareness and your emotional response? What happens when you make a memory more colourful or allow it to pale?

Another great range of possible differences is cultural. White may be the colour of pure spirituality in the West. In China, people who mourn dress in white, and to bear a white blossom or ornament in the hair is said to be unlucky. Some Eastern religions even imagine 'the void' as white, while most Westerners would tend to imagine it as black. The 'healing powers of the white light', sold by countless positive thinkers to their zombie apprentices in Europe and America, might seriously disturb a Chinese whose deep mind contains the belief that white connects with death and emptiness. Of course I would not deny that white light can heal, provided white happens to mean 'healing' to you.

How can we find out what the colours mean to us? In the old aeon, a so-called master would decide what the colours meant. These inspirations would probably be assumed to be valid for all people and as far as the master was concerned, they were valid and they worked. To the eager followers of the master, things were not quite as easy. Those whose minds resembled that of their master could probably get good results using the same colour code, and would continue the tradition with followers who resembled them. The ones who couldn't make it work were usually told that it's all their own fault. What they really needed was a tradition more suited to their nature and in which everyone develops her or his own methods. To hell with tradition: you are unique!

Exercise three - what colours may reveal

Here are some experiments which may reveal what the colours mean to you.

1. This is for people who can imagine colours easily. Make yourself comfortable and go into a gentle and relaxed trance state. Imagine a colour. Focus on it, speak of it in your inner voice, feel it as if it had substance, texture and density. Imagine that you are being surrounded by the colour. Make the experience as vivid as you can. How do you react to the colour? What ideas come into your mind? How do you feel? What emotions arise? Just when and where could these emotions be of use to you? When you have had enough, allow the colour to evaporate. Take a deep breath and open your eyes. This works much like the bell in ritual: it marks the end of one unit and the beginning of the next. Close them again and try the next colour.

2. Some find this easier when done in the style of astral projection. Imagine you are standing before a doorway. The passage is veiled by a thick cloth curtain, which is in the colour which you wish to learn about. Take your time. Look at the colour, feel the cloth, hear yourself speaking of the colour. Tell yourself that there is an entire world in that colour, and that you can enter it through the curtain. When you are ready, open the curtain and walk through. It may be that you'll require several doors and curtains before you arrive in the world of the colour, the world your deep mind has created to represent the meaning of the colour to you. When you have learned enough, return the way you came and be careful to close the various curtains as you leave.

3. Now we'll try memories. In your light trance, close your eyes and select a recent memory, which is still fresh on your mind. Use associated perception. Remember it carefully. Choose a colour. Now go through the memory giving it that colour. You could imagine that you are seeing through coloured lenses, that the place or event is illuminated by strong coloured lights, or that the air itself has colour.

When you have run through the memory in that colour, dissolve the colour, open and close your eyes and repeat using another colour. You will notice that the mood of the memory changes. Some colours and some memories fit, while others make the scene unreal. Try it with several sorts of memories, and make notes. Try an unhappy memory. Which colours make it seem absurd, and allow you to dissociate the emotional impact? Which colours make you feel indifferent, which colours make you feel better?

Remember a magical working you enjoyed. Which colours would increase its radiation? Remember what you look like. What would you look like, surrounded by an aura of various colours? Associate with the vision, find out by living it.

4. Find out in daily life. How does your awareness change when you imagine some coloured aura-radiation around yourself? What is each colour good for?

5. Experiment with fine details. How many shades of each colour can you imagine? Which degrees excite you, which soothe, and which come in handy in everyday life.

Chapter Seven
Imagination and Prayer

You may have learned that your awareness can be changed when you move attention from one sensory channel to the other. You may have noticed that you can speak of your experience, and that the modulation of your voice, its tempo, rhythm and emphasis, can change this experience, leading to all sorts of interesting consciousness states. To some of you, this may have been a surprising discovery. We all have learned to speak and listen. We have also learned, for some obscure reason, to pay a lot of attention to the meaning of words, and to disregard the way that they are spoken. Very few people in our culture pay attention to voice modulation, which seems a great waste of valid information to me. Studies on brain mechanisms indicate that there are several sorts of information involved in spoken messages. Some parts of the brain (usually in the left hemisphere) are good at understanding the meaning of the words, while parts of the other hemisphere respond to tempo, modulation, energy tonus and so on. In many people, this division of understanding is aligned with conscious and unconscious functioning. In our culture, most people learn to focus information, on meaning, on contents (this is the 'what') while disregarding the way the message is transmitted (the 'how').

Consider prayer and invocation. One common mistake is to handle invocation the way you would hold a reasonable discussion. The words must be right. The names of power must come from some genuine source. Divine names—and only the right ones—are read or recited. Often enough we want to make everything so perfect that speaking becomes a difficult task indeed. The solution for this is writing invocations and memorizing them, provided we don't use a classical prayer from the start, some exalted words in old Egyptian, Sumerian, proto-Celtic or medieval Icelandic.

All of this sounds impressive. Aren't the traditional words the ones that work the magick? Isn't there amazing power in the old and hopefully genuine names of the gods? I've heard some witches claiming that anyone who lacks their true and traditional god-names cannot be a genuine witch, as only the true, and (of course) secret names, provide genuine contact to the true and genuine gods. I've heard young Wiccans reciting long lists of god names to 'raise power', (more names to raise more power), no matter that they didn't understand a third of what they were calling. What about the classical methods?

The better sort of practising magicians (the ones who really practice) learned long ago that an invocation, even if the meaning is right, does not amount to much if it is voiced in a dull or everyday modulation. Members of the Hermetic Order of the Golden Dawn *et al* developed a sonorous, dramatic way of 'vibrating the words'. To get into the right mood the mage recites all sorts of stuff to strengthen self-confidence (such as names, titles and achievements). The invocation follows, in a voice that shakes the earth and carries to the limits of the universe, and this voice is made as impressive and dramatic as possible. Using this voice we get a lot of effects which we didn't when we merely spoke in the everyday-small-talk voice. It's a sad fact that most mages stop there.

I once listened to a tape of self-styled king of the witches, Alex Sanders. I found the first ten minutes of his invocation well done and dramatic. After fifteen minutes I began to feel bored. Another five minutes later the spirit of Loki began to make nasty remarks in the deep of my mind, snappy comments on those who learn one technique which works and never bother to learn another. It doesn't matter how good a 'ritual voice' may be: if used for too long, the effect wears off and attention wanders elsewhere.

We have seen what happens when we emphasize the 'what', disregarding the 'how'. Now there is another approach to invocation, which emphasizes the 'how' to such an extent that the conscious mind, with its love for the 'what', can get pretty upset. This is the case with Enochian invocations, with the 'barbarous names' and such practices as 'chanting in chaos language'. Here attention goes very much into sound, loudness, modulation, as the words which are 'said' don't make any sense to the conscious mind. What they lack in meaning they make up for in power. It seems hardly surprising that most beginners feel very uneasy about them. The degree of resistance may tell us something about the obsessive need of the ego to 'be in control'.

If you want real changes in your awareness, how about a mixed program? You might start out in a meaningful invocation of this or that, then switch to chaos language allowing wild and wonderful words to form themselves, and fall into chanting and dancing to raise a lot of power. Then might follow the next unit of speech in meaningful prose, and so on. You will realize that this sort of ritual activates a good many parts of the mind which would lie latent (and bored) in a traditional dignified ceremony which pleases the conscious mind and very little else. The same goes for other branches of invocation, such as hypnosis, trance induction, story telling or reciting poetry.

There are people who claim that a good hypnotherapist should always speak in a slow, deep and monotonous voice. This will work wonders if you want to induce slow, deep and monotonous trances. Do this with yourself and you may find yourself falling asleep. The better sort of hypnotherapists, such as Milton Erickson, made an art of the use of pauses. Others use whispering. When you whisper your suggestions, your client will have to listen more closely, and the attention may even increase, as we all know that it is the important and very secret things that get expressed in such a voice. In some trances, we may even require a wild and exciting voice.

If we want to contact the spirit of love, for instance we can please our conscious minds with ceremonial prayer to the right sort of deities, such as Venus, Vanadis, Fria, Ishtar, Inanna, Erzulie (Voodoo goddess of love) or Babalon. No doubt we can easily choose one of these who will feel natural, and with a little research we may find a lot of symbols and mythology to supply our conscious mind with meanings to get the prayer going. All of these, no matter how finely worked out, won't amount to anything unless we call with power and passion, which will require (for the start) a loving attitude, and a loving sort of voice, to make contact with the spirit of love. There are a good many gods and spirits who care very little for the meaning of the invocation and respond much faster to its mood. This is especially the case with the elder gods, the ancient ones and those primal spirits of the dawn ages who don't give a damn for reason anyway.

Cup meditation

Here is a practice of the most elementary sort. At least, this is what I assumed it to be when I learned it from two friends who had received it from a Yoruba priest. Indeed I almost considered it too easy at first. My friends had been told that it is a method of prayer. This is a good description, though not the only one. When I teach it to people who don't like the idea of 'prayer' I call it an 'exercise in congruent speech and vivid imagination'. The practice is based on the eucharist, force and sentience are invoked, charged into a cup of fluid, which is poured as a libation and drunk to integrate the energy.

What you need is simply two cups, horns or drinking vessels, and some of you may find this working easier when only two special vessels are used, consecrated vessels that are dedicated only to ritual use. As a fluid, we may use water which will change in taste during the working, or wine, or stronger spirits such as gin or rum. If you are familiar with ritual, give this exercise the ceremonial beginning you are used to. If you are not, and feel uneasy about it, simply make yourself comfortable. Relax, take a few deep breaths and sit for a minute or three in silence, so your mind can prepare itself for the good things to follow.

Transformations

Hold one cup in each hand, the right hand cup should be filled (with a liquid of your choice), the left hand cup is empty. As you hold your cups you pray, call and evoke. You can invoke any sort of force and sentience. When you sense it strongly—your imagination does this—bring the vision into the fluid. If you have evoked fire, for example, you should 'enflame yourself with prayer'. When you have become fiery and wild, feeling warm or hot, with sparkling eyes and fierce laughter, and your imagination has filled the entire room with burning, living flame, make the vision smaller and more intense until it fills the fluid in your right hand cup with its power.

Each time you have charged the fluid with some force or sentience, pour some of it into the left hand cup. Then invoke the next item, and pour that, and so on, until the left hand cup is full and the right hand cup is empty. Now you will be holding a cup full of blessings in your left hand. Pour it into the right and vice versa a couple of times, until all ideas of your invocation are well mixed. Then pour a libation to the gods and spirits of your mind and sprinkle some of the fluid around in your room: wherever the drops fall they will consecrate the atmosphere. Give your thanks and drink the rest. This will transform you from within.

Of course this description is not complete. A good many of you will ask 'but what should I call and how?' Imagine that you want to invoke the four (or five) elements earth, air, fire, water and spirit. Most of you will be familiar with this model of the universe. Of course you might just as well invoke the planetary forces, the sephira, your favourite god forms, or any other force or being that suits you. In Africa, I would like to add, they do not invoke the elements as we know them, but the gods and spirits each mage is in touch with.

Invoking the elements

If you would invoke the elements, you might begin with earth, and this is how your speech might sound. Do yourself a favour and speak aloud. I know that many would rather 'pray silently' or 'work this entirely in the imagination'. It was the same with me—the usual reluctance to speak freely in case we say something 'wrong'. Well, in this practice, you can't say anything wrong. It's your deep mind which will supply the ideas and the words. The vital issue is that you dare to open your mouth and start speaking.

Invoking earth: an example:

This is the first stage: We describe what we are calling:

Hear me. . . as I call. . . and invoke. . . the force of earth. . . strong earth. . . fertile earth. . . solid ground. . . I call to you! Earth of the fields. . . Mother of grain. . . giver of food. . . solid earth. . . peaceful earth. . . I call to you come to the rite. . . come to the working. . . ground and soil. . . dust and dirt. . . source of all life. . . giver of flesh. . . Be ye with us! By field and meadow. . . by rock and stone. . . by hill and mountain. . . fruitful earth. . . joyous earth. . . heavy earth and damp and rich brown. . . in many colours. . . I can feel your weight. . . and your density. . . the strength of the rocks. . . the age old patience. . . of the stones. . . and the crystals. . . as they rest. . . and sleep. . . and dream.

Here we emphasis our unity with earth:

Earth. . . you are here. . . I feel your touch. . . your depth. . . your strength. . . I can see you. . . in my mind. . . the mountains. . . the fields. . . the plains. . . even deserts. . . I remember. . . what earth. . . means to me. . . and there is earth. . . in my body. . . all flesh. . . is earth. . . is matter. . . is form. . . I feel my body. . . feel the cups. . . the rocks. . . are like bone. . . they are firm. . . and solid. . . I feel my flesh. . . resting quietly. . . my flesh. . . all flesh. . . grown out of earth. . . returning to earth. . . the density. . . the weight. . . the firmness. . . the duration. . . all earth. . . one earth. . .

This is stage three: We speak for the earth.

This earth. . . is of myself. . . and by giving life. . . by living. . . I embody earth. . . become the sentience. . . I am the consciousness. . . of all earth. . . all life. . . grows out of my body. . . finds form. . . and food. . . out of myself. . . I am eternal earth. . . I change. . . and I remain. . . all form. . . arises out of me.

If you manage to describe what you are calling, and to speak freely, and spontaneously for a while, you are doing well. Some do this by remembering. When you remember the many experiences you have had with earth, you will have a lot of material to describe. When you describe it vividly—what do you feel? What do you see? What do you hear and taste and smell? The description will become quite lively. You will describe what you experience and experience what you describe, soon enough your imagination will go into overdrive and then—this is when the magick takes off—you will be so enthusiastic it will carry you away.

When your imagination of earth is vivid and you feel its qualities and moods, charge the fluid with it. Pour all the visions, thoughts and feelings of your earth into the liquid until it brims with solidity, firmness, density and duration. Then pour a little into the left hand cup and proceed with water.

Again, you might speak of your memories, speak of rain and snow, river and stream, lake and pool, mist and clouds, and the open sea. You might speak of the waters that flow in your body, that circulate in the blood, the waters that feed and clean the cells, the waters that carry the hormones, that give the tides of emotion to our minds. And you might speak as the eternal sea out of which all life came. . . but I won't have to tell you more, you know it anyway. Fire and air follow in the same fashion, and for spirit, I hope you improvise something such as a fit of laughter.

So much for the contents. Now for the mood. Just as important as what you say is how you say it. You will find that an invocation of earth sounds much more convincing when it is spoken in an earthy voice. To me, the earth voice is deep and sonorous. It sounds firm and slow, and sometimes when I get very earthy it gets very slow indeed. What would it sound to you? Each of the elements has its own special voice. The water voice, for instance, tends to sway and surge and pulse, it has a

A Weaver

regular or rhythmic flow, and some sounds, especially the 's', 'sh' and 'z' can be emphasized. The fire voice can be wild and fierce. It erupts suddenly, then calms, then roars out again. Rant and rave if you can: Fire is wild and so are you. The air voice is calmer. It tends to breathe, to sigh, to howl, to whistle and to whisper like the wind, and sometimes words die out and all one does is to breathe in great, joyous gusts. The spirit voice will be something personal to you.

Consider—Would you invoke all elements in the same sort of voice? This would certainly sound dull, especially if the rite takes half an hour or more. Also, you would communicate your ideas only to those parts of the brain which understand the abstract symbolism of words. Now the modulation of the voice is just as meaningful as the words that are said, only that it activates different parts of the mind. An invocation is only effective when it really makes you experience what you are talking about: it is this experience, your identity with the invoked force, that makes the rite valid. It doesn't matter what you say for example, about fire: the trick is to become so fiery that the force burns you up. This is why I called this prayer method an exercise in congruence.

Usually I ask beginners to get used to this practice by praying once daily for at least two weeks. Probably two weeks won't suffice, but at least they will be ready for group sessions by then. In group workings, the two cups are given to each participant, who is free to invoke what s/he wills, as it happens. The other participants may amplify the prayer by adding appropriate sounds. We might use a deep, slow drum for earth, and add some flutes and horns for air to get it going. Click sticks may be useful to simulate the crackle of fire and sloshing water around in a bowl may amplify the mood of the fluid element.

The cup meditation in a group

Here is something for those of you who have practised the elements prayer for a while. Meet some of your like-minded friends. Now sit down with the cups as usual and invoke the usual program, but do it in chaos language. No reasonable words or names please! Simply produce sounds, noises, chaos words, chant and song. When two or more people do this at once, they will weave a fabric of sound which may come to vivid life.

With earth, this may mean deep, droning voices, vibrating and singing sounds like 'm' , 'n' , 'o' , 'u' in a regular and slow pattern. With water it might be the sound of the waves as they surge, the screams of the gulls, the falling of drops, the hissing, slurping sounds of fluids that hiss and flow and gurgle. With fire we get the dry crack of the wood, the small explosions, and a lot of screaming, roaring and shouting, full of madness and lust, and with air the howl of the wind whistling, sighing, blowing and perhaps wide vowels to be sung, such as the 'a' and 'e'.

Don't worry about my hopeless attempts to explain chaotic sounds; try it out, you may find that your contact to the elements does not really require words, and that the chaotic sounds you make touch a very deep and primal level with each element. This may have side effects. You may have noticed that the sort of magick I live for isn't very dignified. This has a valid reason. There are lots of mages who work ceremony and try to look dignified, or exalted or spiritual or whatever. Usually it means that they look pompous and stiff.

The mages of the last centuries have established the curious idea that a real mage ought to be fully in control, ought to bow before god while bossing spirits in triangles. It hardly mattered what they invoked as it always sounded the same anyway. This mask they assumed comes from organized religion. It is the role of the serene high priest which they played, the giver of law, justice and belief, the sacred authority, aloof and serene. Of course such a priest, who has to represent an organized religion is in no position to crack jokes or make errors.

Consider the shamans—it is part of their activity that they get so excited by their magick that they become wild and enthusiastic until the spirits arise and obsess them. Now each spirit requires a different sort of enthusiasm, meaning that the shaman has to be quite flexible. Also, the spirits, once they incarnate, are out to enjoy themselves. Most of them don't care what the common people think or say, and some of them may even love to annoy, provoke or insult. All of this would be quite impossible if the shaman would insist on 'being in control', on looking dignified or trying to keep the robe clean. When the wild-boar spirit gets you, you might discover that you enjoy to snort around on the ground, and when it's the serpent, you might become lithe, and sexy and very poisonous.

The same may be said of the elements. The usual ceremonial mage is not congruent with any of them, but tries to be their master - lets do this differently. With earth we become strong and heavy, with water, the body may sway and pulse, with fire, heat and sweat may appear, and wild screaming, while air may inspire songs or breathing exercises, as it happens. We want to experience what we invoke, to express the power and the sentience in living flesh.

For our prayer exercise we get carried away. You are doing well when you forget about control and dignity and become what you are speaking with. If you should shudder, tremble, shake, vibrate or jerk during prayer, don't be alarmed: it's only a Seidr (seething) trance taking place. Such phenomena used to be normal in the older European nature religions (before an organized priesthood began to insist on dignity). They are a good sign that bio-energies are flowing, that power is released, both in the emotional and the sexual sense.

This power is vital for magick, quite probably it is this energy which is required by the gods and spirits to manifest in. More on seething and energy magick will be found in my books *Helrunar* and *Seidways*. For now it should suffice to say that a good mage works passionately. A good invocation is not just a well-worded intellectual mind game. It should catch you and grip you with the whole of your being. If you can do that, if you can begin to pray and then find that you've been in action for an hour, when you are well versed with this prayer, you may use it for anything.

For example: thanksgiving, when you feel good and want to share it. Problem solving, when you feel lost and want to discuss your situation with the gods or spirits. Union, when you want to have a drink with all the other aspects of yourself. Consecration, when you charge

Worm of Hell

the fluid and use it to anoint or heal. Transformation, when you ask the self aspects (gods, spirits, elements) to change you from within. Given enough flexibility, you may make this simple little ritual one of the most vital methods for all sorts of magick.

So, if you find yourself swaying, or shaking, or sweating or screaming, or if mad impulses get you, or you begin to rant in chaos-language, you are doing fine. A great deal of the deeper sort of magick gets done by parts of the deep mind which have their own laws and reasons, many of which will seem 'insane' or 'crazy' to the conscious mind. Once we begin to release and integrate what lies hidden in our depths, we will find that control is not needed and that true dignity is not achieved by being stiff and pompous.

Chapter Eight
Mandala Building

Imagine, Munich, June 1989. From Kathmandu, a group of three Tibetan monks arrive, the honourable Lobsang Tinle, Lobsang Palden and Lobsang Thardo. The next day the three begin to build a mandala in the local Buddhist centre.

A mandala is a map, a model of the world, a model of the mind, and a powerful visual device to invoke specific consciousness states. Like sigils and symbols, mandalas touch the deeper layers of the mind.

The ritual begins early. First, the spirits of the house are called and asked to provide space, and to give their blessing to the ceremony. Then the entire house and all participants are purified. Incense is burned, prayers are chanted and sacrificial gifts are offered to the spirits of house and neighbourhood. Now Avalokateshvara is invoked, the spirit of love and compassion for whom the mandala will be built. The monks open their prayer books and begin to recite their mantras in deep, droning voices, ringing their bells and weaving a fabric of sound to attune them to their work. As the monks sense that Avalokateshvara gives permission, the chants fade and the measuring begins. On a large plinth of wood the mandala is drawn, the circles, squares, lotus flowers and geometrical structures that bind the whole. Seated in their lotus postures and leaning over the wood, the monks begin to fill in the colours. This is done by pouring coloured sand through long metalsnouted tools. The work is time consuming and requires a very steady hand. Layer upon layer is poured, large spaces and small symbols, garlands, ornaments, flowers and syllables. In the middle is the sign of Avalokateshvara, whose palace the mandala will become. It is a small flowery shape in red, white and yellow atop a circle in light green. Around the circle flowers a large lotus of eight leaves: four red, two yellow, one blue and one in green, each surrounded by a rim in white. Around the circle shape of the lotus a square is formed, which is coloured in yellow, blue, green and white. Then follow several bands of fine ornaments, and circles radiant in rainbow splendour. These are framed by a much larger square which has the same colours as the smaller one.

For ten days the monks are busy with their mandala, caring very little for the numerous observers, the curious, the new-agers or the TV-team. From time to time they look up and laugh. What the monks are doing here, for the first time in public, is part of the ritual tradition of their home country. The building of the sacred diagram is a gesture for the world.

Imagine, in the highlands of Bolivia, a peasant has called for the local sorcerer, one of the few remaining Callawaya healers. The healer arrives in the evening, carrying a large bundle of ritual objects. The patient hasn't been well for months. Disease, weakness, poverty and ill-luck. . . all of these will be cured by the Callawaya. The patient speaks of his pains and fears. Has he done wrong? Has he upset the gods or spirits? Have the evil creatures of the night snatched his soul away? The healer listens, comforts, consults an oracle. As is usually the case, a *Mesa* (Spanish: table) is prepared. As the Callawayas have it, 'a mesa is good for everything'. This begins by spreading a large, whitish cloth over a crate. Praying aloud, the healer lays out twelve small squares of paper, each of them folded at the edges to make it a container. The squares are laid out with great precision. Some healers place them in a rectangular arrangement, some form groups and others form a circle, depending on the tradition of their home village.

Though the Callawayas travel for hundreds of miles in their work, most of them stick to the tradition they grew up with, and insist it is the only method which works. Into each paper square a ball of cotton is given, which is carefully formed like a nest. Praying continuously, the Callawaya decorates each nest with coca-leaves, adding flowers, blossoms, sweets, bits of fruit, small leaden figures and other items, depending very much on what the patient can afford. An egg is greased with llama fat: the traditional offering for the Ankari: the messenger spirit, who will carry the message of the Mesa to the otherworld. Not all nests are alike. Each of them is dedicated to another agency, being or desire. Some are for the house spirits, some for the Catholic heaven, the god of thunder and lightning, some for dangerous or ill-tempered spirits, and some for the ancient places of power, the sacred mountains of the Andes. The patients usually know which sacred mountain is their guardian, even if that mountain should be hundreds of miles away.

For hours the voice of the healer rings through the night. A llama foetus is decorated with flowers, greased with fat, laid out as an offering. Healing is asked for, and forgiveness. Bolivian Indians tend to live in catastrophic worlds full of evil-minded spirits, most of whom demand regular offerings and recognition. In such a belief system it can be dangerous to forget a sacrifice. To make sure, the healer calls to all spirits, be they known or unknown, recognized or forgotten, to forgive all known and unknown misdeeds of the patient, to partake of the offering and to send blessings to the patient and healer, and all persons who might be present.

When the Mesa is complete, the ritual comes to a climax. The Callawaya charges and dedicates a cup full of strong alcohol and pours it over the Mesa and around the hut, purifying and consecrating the ritual space and its contents. Now comes a pause. For half an hour or more the patient and the healer sit together, chatting, smoking, drinking and laughing. The Mesa is ignored for a while. Like a sigil, it needs time and forgetfulness to work. Later in the night, the ritual continues. Incense is burned, the patient is purified and a bell is sounded. Last of all, the entire Mesa is burned, transformed by fire, until none of the original ingredients can be recognized. Often the healer does the burning on his own. Many Callawayas believe that it can be dangerous for the patient to see the Mesa burning. The same goes for any other person who might happen to pass by.

Mandala building is a method that can be found in many traditions. A mandala can be seen as a 'sacred alignment', a description of the inner and outer universe (made perfect), a prayer in visual form.

When we lay out a Magick circle or decorate the altar, we are creating such a map of the inner and outer universe. In a ritual circle, each item represents an aspect of ourselves. The tools of our working are not simply tossed into a heap near the altar, they are laid out with care and consideration, so that the altar decoration itself is a map for the self-aspects which will join in the working.

A good layout is at once balanced, simple and complex. As we work in the 'artificial' reality of the circle, we are free to make the circle a good world to be in. The altar and temple decoration is often meant to show the world in a balanced and healed state, an ideal world just as it ought to be. This 'perfect mandala' becomes a powerful suggestion.

The same principles are often at work in daily life. Many people feel a periodic need to redecorate their homes, especially in times of crisis and change, so that the realignment of the inner finds reflection or reinforcement in the outer. Some find that housework, such as cleaning and redecoration, has a calming effect on the mind. For such people, housework is a ritual which seriously influences their consciousness. Others focus on a neat and clean living space not so much to support an inner change of consciousness, but to evade the necessity to do something for their inner world. Personally, I suspect that the people with a balanced and healthy inner life have too much to do enjoying life to waste time keeping their homes perfect. No doubt you have built many mandalas in your daily life, ritual alignments of many varieties, even if you were not aware of it. Cleaning the home, laying out the breakfast table, getting some sort of order into the books and records, each of these activities may involve mandala building. Most of them go beyond the practical and into the artistic: the arrangement invokes a specific sort of consciousness. It obviously follows that we may make good use of this natural trait, try out some new forms of alignment and enjoy what happens.

A personal mandala

One mandala well worth the effort will be described next. Once a year, usually at Lammas/Lughnasad in early August, I go out into the fields and forests to build a hoop of plants which are tough, long and flexible. Mugwort is very good for this, 'mug' means 'might' indicating that the plant will last and endure. Other items for the frame are the branches and twigs of birch and willow, which will bend and dry well.

Once the hoop is formed, many other plants are added. Some grains can still be found in August, these symbolize the nourishment of the year to come. Then there are other plants. The hoop of last year, which is hanging before me now, is decorated with bundles of oats, wheat and rye. There are clusters of fir cones, hazelnuts, chestnuts, dried and shrivelled rowan berries, thistles, hedgerow berries, yarrow flowers, whitethorn leaves and berries, oak leaves and a couple of smaller plants that defy identification. Also bound into the arrangement are feathers of forest birds, boar bristles, deer hair and a couple of small bones. All of these are gifts. Nature offers them freely to all who bother to recognize and enjoy them.

From August to Winter all sorts of materials come my way, and these are bound and integrated in the round. Each item is consecrated. I speak of, with and about it as I cut or collect it, and give it a goodly dose of prayer when it gets bound. This connects each item with a specific memory, and gives it a purpose and meaning in the whole. The hoop itself symbolizes the yearly cycle of nature. When the leaves fall and the weather gets gloomy and cold, the hoop at home carries the joy and promise of fresh life all through the winter time.

The ritual, as far as we may call it that, consists of prayer. Speak with plants (loud and clear). You may fell silly. Keep in mind the word comes from old high German 'saelig', meaning blessed. Speaking with the plants should be familiar to all who have read Castaneda. The plants may not understand the words but they will understand your voice modulation and the mood you are in. Some plants ought to be asked for permission. They will find a way of telling you what and how much you may take. Speak with the plants that you gather. Tell them what you are collecting them for. Describe their shape, meaning and symbolism, and ask them to come with you. When the next Lughnasad feast comes, a new hoop is bound, and the old one, with all its dried herbs and flowers gets burned.

Alternatively, I start out by going to the forest. There I pray to the gods and spirits that they may send good material for the mandala. During the day I collect them. A couple of twigs here, some dry leaves there, small cones, fir branches, fern leaves and whatever comes my way. As each item is gathered, I speak with the spirit of that plant, tell it the purpose of the rite and ask for its blessing. At home they are sorted out.

I place a large brass plate atop a wooden tripod. A large stone would do just as well; the important item is the metal plate. Taking one sort of plant growth after the other, I pray. Leaves, for example, can symbolize the power to die and be reborn. Roots might be used as a symbol for earth, firmness and duration. Fir twigs might symbolize life that continues all through the year, nuts and seeds, hidden life and new life to be.

You'll find more symbolism later on. The important symbolism, the meaning of each plant to you, is what makes the magick work. You will discover this symbolism through practice. It's part of the fun to take up some time and to start praying. This may easily lead to all sorts of amusing trance states, provided you really start speaking and get carried away by it. Each item, once its power and meaning is invoked, is placed on the metal plate. If you like to you can make the plate your mandala. An example of a layout is illustrated. Given a basic nine items, we can be busy calling, praying and invoking for an hour. This may seem awfully long for those who find it hard to voice three clear words in a ritual, but have no problems chatting of all sorts of everyday topics for

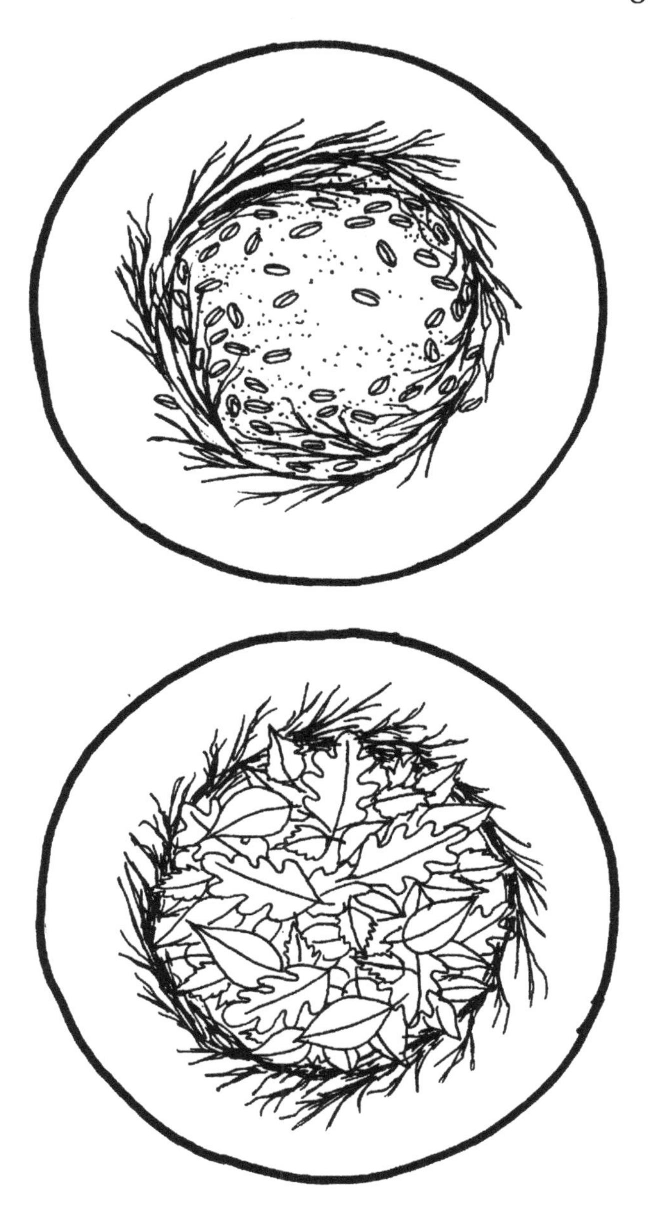

Building a Mandala - using salt, grains, roots, leaves, spruce twigs, fir cones and berries

hours. In the end the metal plate will be decorated with a lavish heap of well-arranged floral growth. Now I consecrate the mandala as a whole. Using the prayer method of the last chapter, I call and invoke who or whatever seems appropriate into the fluid, and soak both the mandala and the room with it. The rest is drunk, to work from within.

The rest of the working follows the Callawaya method. I give myself a pause to eat, drink, dance or make music, while the mandala lurks quietly in its corner and has time 'to sink in'. After a while the prayer continues. As a last act, the mandala is drenched with pure alcohol and burned. The leftovers and ashes are buried the next day.

The offering acts like a sigil. It is collected, gathered, aligned, dedicated, blessed, burned and forgotten. Like a sigil, the mandala speaks a strong message to the deep mind. Unlike the sigil working, the mandala offering involves a long walk in nature, plus plenty of doing, praying, handling of material objects and such, which makes the magick more practical. The act of prayer releases pressure and tension—it can be useful to exhaust oneself with prayer—and helps to gather ideas, visions, symbols and imagination in word and deed. The many messages collect in a single, ordered form, the mandala. This message is burned, releasing the gathered forces in a single act. As no energy can ever be lost, the ideas which were bound to the plants will find new form to manifest in.

Connecting ideas to the plants

In the Medieval ages, healers believed that each plant shows its virtues through signatures. 'Nature signs each growth that arises to show what it is good for' wrote Paracelsus, 'The form of the corpus evolves out of the inner form of the arcane'. For example, if you will to make a mandala of the four elements, you may select your materials as follows:

For the **EARTH** you might select roots, as they grow in the ground. Dry old mushrooms, as they live low on the ground. Grains, berries and other foodstuffs, as they can symbolize the food for our own earth (body).

Building a Mandala

For **WATER** you might select plants that grow in or near it. Willow, Alder and Poplar would be a good selection. Also fresh green plants with plenty of sap.

FIRE might be symbolized by blossoms, as they are the sexual organs of plants, often show strong colours, and as science tells us, the blossoms are actually warmer than the rest of the plant. Tinder mushroom, birch bark and fir cones, as these were often used to start fires with, thistles and thorns as symbolize the power to fight.

AIR might be represented by leaves and needles, as these are the lungs of the plants. Thin grasses that sway in the wind. Berries as food for the birds and promise of the plants to come. Mistletoe and other parasites as they grow high above the earth.

Colour may also supply symbolism.

Tree and plant lore

There is a lot of lore connected to the plants and herbs. Many plants were considered sacred to some deity or other, so that parts of these could be used to contact and invoke the gods. The sacred plants of Greece and Rome are well known and described in the Classics. The holy herbs of the northern lands are less well known, which may be due to the persecution inflicted on all pagans between 800 and 1700AD. During the witch hunt a good many plants received new names, so that a lot of old symbolism is lost to us. I will now list some of those sacred plants.

It is perhaps the tree which received most veneration. The last Ice-Age ended between 10,000-8,000BC, depending on location. As the ice-sheet withdrew, it left behind a well-polished terrain of flat wasteland. The country in middle Europe looked much like Northern Scandinavia nowadays: miles and miles of empty Tundra. In winter, the snowstorms howled across the wasteland, in spring, the melting snow turned the land into a swamp. Few people survived in this climate, small groups of nomads living on reindeer, small animals, berries, fish and lichen. The first trees to populate the Tundra were small and tough.

BIRCH. The tree to symbolize the beginning. Popular in countless spring festivities all over the world. Sacred to the spring goddesses, such as Ostara/Oestre, the birch symbolizes the rebirth of light and fresh life. The leaves make an excellent tea which cleanses the body, washes toxins and waste out and helps against rheumatism and arthritis.

ROWAN. The original world-ash, long before ash trees were known, was probably a rowan tree. This connects it with the ancestral shaman, with the god forms of Wodan and Odin. Atop the tree, between heaven and earth, Odin saw the runes and took them up screaming—and where could he have seen them, if not in the shape of the branches? The rowan is one of the most popular trees if one wants to drive evil spirits away. The leaves provide a good tea which helps against diarrhoea, the blossoms are good against diseases of the lungs, the berries help against scurvy.

WILLOW. The classical witches' tree. Some connect willows with the Norns ('Nyrnir' = weavers), who bind fate and weave reality. Willow branches were often woven to make baskets or furniture. The willow can live in and near water. As the saying goes 'where the disease originates, the cure can be found'. Willows, leaves and bark, are a wonderful remedy for colds and fevers. They induce strong sweating while reducing the pain. It was custom to ask the willow tree that supplied the medicine to accept and hold the disease.

ALDER. Another tree of the swampland, the alder survives with the help of small mushrooms and fungi which protect the roots from decay. Alders can grow in water, and quite probably the alder was one of the trees that turned the swampland into firm ground. Robert Graves connects the alder with the cult of Bran. Continental mythology sees the alder as a tree of the great goddess, out of whom both sexes, symbolized by the two sorts of fruit, came forth.

Alders are known to bleed red sap when they are cut. The bark was soaked in water, with some iron, to produce a good black colour. The alder is the home of a spirit or deity called 'Fru Arle', 'Else' or 'Irle' who waits and lurks in the swamp. Lonesome travellers meet her on occasion, and are driven barmy. Appearing as a mix between a lovely maiden and a coarse monster, Ms Else asks them to marry her. What follows, as the legends reveal, are endless attempts to flee the swamp, during which our poor wanderer gets a heady attack of swamp fever. The cure is to accept her. The swamp gives the fever and the alder takes it away. This is how the bark was used for medicine.

FIR and **SPRUCE** survived the ice ages atop the mountain ranges. These evergreen trees were held sacred in many rituals. The legend goes that god sought shelter under a spruce. The tree kept him safe and dry, and as a small gesture of thanks, received evergreen twigs. The spruce was one on the few sources of vitamin C in the old days. Studies show that the content of vitamin C is lowest in summer, but rises to reach its height in midwinter. Though the tea tasted unpleasant it was one on the few cures against scurvy, apart from the use of the essential oil to heal bronchitis and diseases of the lungs.

In southern Germany, the spruce is used as a May tree. Most of the bark is stripped, as are the branches, so that only a long, straight pole remains with green twigs at the top. This tree is decorated with foodstuff and long colourful ribbons which are twisted around it during the May-dance. Spruces were sometimes held sacred to the gods of the ocean, as they make good masts.

POPLARS were also among the first trees. A clear mythological meaning was probably lost. One hears that the German priests used to burn the leaves as incense, and to chew the buds which is supposed to be psychoactive but taste godawful.

During the next couple of millennia, the weather got warmer and the swampland turned into firm ground. By 7000BC, the countryside is populated with vast forests of birch and hazel.

HAZEL. This tree, or shrub, supplied the first nuts known in the North. In the *Edda*, we may read how Iduna, the goddess of life and youth is caught by the frost giant Thiassi. Loki steals her out of Thiassi's keep. In the shape of a nut he carries Iduna across the frozen wasteland, returning the force of life to the Aesir.

Iro-Celtic mythology speaks of a 'salmon of knowledge'. This enchanted beast obtained its fabulous wisdom by eating the hazelnuts of knowledge that grew near the shore. All sorts of magick wands used to be made out of hazel twigs. The church never really liked the hazel. To them, as to the common people, the hazel was a symbol of lust and carnal pleasure.

By 5000BC the larger sort of trees began to cover the land.

ASH. In the Germanic tradition, this tree became representative of all trees that exist, the world tree which connects heaven and earth and nourishes all beings. The *Edda* tells us that the first humans, Ask and Embla, were created out of an ash and an alder.

OAK. Nowadays a symbol for 'the sacred tree' or the 'tree of the Druids', this tree has received more publicity than it deserves. The oak was the sacred tree of the ancient sky god, be he called Twisto, Tiwaz, Thor, Donar, Taranis or Zeus. It is also a tree of the warriors. The oak has to resist more parasites than any other tree. A powder of the bark was used to disinfect and close wounds. Then there are the leaves. The oak is one of the last trees to 'wake up' in the spring, but once it has its leaves, it will retain them longer than any other. This made the oak a symbol for endurance. Oak trees were often used for lawgiving or judgment, the people gathering under the vast branches, where the god of the heavens, wielder of thunder and lightning, could be close to them.

LIME. Perhaps the most popular of the northern trees, the lime was often planted in the centre of the village, as it was known to bring love and harmony. The linden tree was dedicated to Fria or Freya ('the beloved one'), goddess of love and beauty, a belief which the church speedily changed into the 'Maria-Lime'. The blossoms are a good medicine against fever and cold, as they help the body to sweat the disease out. Connected to the tree is the bee, which produces some of its finest honey out of the flowers. Some old legends tell us that the lime, with its heart-shaped leaves, was often asked to help in matters of love. Whenever this failed, the tree was required to share the suffering. Sometimes the lime would provide a 'divine judgment'. Suspected criminals were allowed to plant a small lime tree with the branches in the earth, the roots towards the sky. If this tree produced leaves among the roots within two years, the goddess had spoken and the suspect was considered innocent.

BEECH. The beech, 'the mother of the forest', has little folklore. As a guess we may consider her sacred to Wodan and the Norns, and to all who carve runes and cast lots. To this day, the German word for 'letter' is Buchstabe, i.e. staff of beech. Some beeches grow in bizarre shapes when the earth-dragon twists them. These, especially the ones with clefts or large holes, could take diseases away. If you are ill you may try it out. Ask the tree to make you whole, then climb through the opening (if need be nine times) and if you are lucky, the tree will free you of your disease.

In spring, the beech shows wonderful green leaves. These leaves, together with the leaves of the birch, were often used to build 'green man' figures. Sometimes a child was dressed in the fresh green foliage, then the 'green man' who represented spring and fresh life, was carried to the village in triumph.

Another sacred tree I would like to introduce you to is the **ELDER**. This graceful shrub likes to grow near houses. In the old times it was frequently planted around the house and garden, mainly for reasons of magick, as it was said to drive the evil spirits away. The elder is called 'Ellhorn', 'holunder' or 'holler' in German, which ought to remind you of Hel, Hella or Helja, the goddess of 'hell', the underworld. Helja devours the dead and prepares them, in her hidden, sacred hollow, for a new lifetime. Sometimes the dead and unborn come back to speak with the living, and if we can trust the evidence of several legends, they like to manifest through the elder tree.

Elder berries were probably used for body-painting, a custom which was fairly popular with some Celtic and Pictish tribes. The blue colour was known to protect. There are many taboos which forbid the cutting of elder trees. If a peasant really had to, the cutting was allowed, provided the evil doer would kneel, pray, and apologize very humbly: 'Lady Ellhorn, please give me of your wood as I will give mine to you, when it grows in the forest'. All parts of the tree, leaves, fruit and blossoms, were used for medicine, to sweat the fever out.

JUNIPER was protected by taboo, just as the elder was. Juniper, used in gin making and all sorts of body-cleaning medicines, was one of the most popular incenses in the north. Custom required that all rooms in the house had to be purified with the smoke several times a year, especially during and after diseases. In the plague years, the well-informed carried smoking juniper branches to ward off the evil spirits. This method certainly works wonders, as juniper wood has disinfecting powers.

The German name Wachholder retains the Indo-European word root *veg meaning 'to weave, to bind', which might remind us of the Norns. Another linguistic explanation focuses on the Wach which means 'awake' or 'quick' in the sense of 'living'. Custom required Tirolean peasants to lift their hats when they passed a juniper tree.

APPLE TREE. The original apple, as it was known to the Celts and Germans, was a tough little thing, hard like wood and very sour. Though it could hardly be eaten, the people loved it, and made it a symbol of life. Iduna, the Nordic goddess of youth and immortality, offers her gifts in the shape of apples. In the legend of Avalon, or Affalon, we encounter another clue, as this other world paradise was named 'Appledale'. Apple-cider became one of those access-routes into the otherworldly ecstatic states of mind. I would like to add that most sorts of fruit, as we know them today, were cultivated and spread by the Romans. Little mythology connects with them, for when the Romans came, much of local pagan religion died out.

YEWS are usually trees of death. They can become very old and tough, with firm wood that can be as old as a thousand years. The best bows were made out of yews, and these bows were so fashionable that the tree is almost extinct today. It survived as a popular cemetery tree 'with one root in each coffin', as the saying goes. Yews were sacred to Ullr, the Nordic god of winter and hunting. As almost all parts of the yew are toxic you would do well not to burn them in your mandala-rite.

THORNS are often signs of giants and monsters. In the old days, thorn bushes were planted around the villages (the English 'thorpe' and the German 'Dorf' contain the word) as a natural protection, to keep evil doers, bandits and (of course) giants outside. Witches used to squat in these bushes, (the German word *Hexe* comes from Hagazussa meaning witch or literally 'hedge-sitter'), between the worlds, in contact with the known and unknown at once.

Smaller plants

Then there were smaller plants sacred to the gods. All blossoms belonged to Nanna in Nordic mythology, as Nanna, wife of the light-god Balder, is blossom herself.

YARROW, bright and radiant, is probably the herb called 'Balder's eyebrow' in the *Edda.*

MISTLETOE connects with Balder (in a relatively painful way), with blind Hod (who didn't see what he was doing) and with Loki, who assures us of his innocence. *The Golden Bough* (see bibliography) describes countless such rites.

DAISIES were dedicated to Ostara, goddess of spring.

PLAINTAIN is called *Wegerich* in German, meaning 'Lord of the Ways', which may refer to Wodan as a traveller.

MUGWORT is a herb dedicated to the goddess in several cultures. It was often used to make birth easier, to heat and relax. In Mediterranean countries the plant was dedicated to Diana and Artemis, who was possibly known as Aradia in Northern Italy, and might correspond with the Celtic bear-goddess Artia.

GRAINS were sacred to several deities,and magical beings such as Bride, Cerridwen, Frey, Freya, Gerda. Jörd, Erke and Granis.

COWSLIP, known as 'Schlüsselblume' (key-flower), was the 'key' for all sorts of magick hills and mountains. To carry the flower was a certain method to find access to the 'kings from under the hill'.

THISTLES and **NETTLES** are Loki's gift to the world. The saying goes: 'I know this herb, said the devil, and relaxed into the nettles'. These plants can symbolize the power to resist.

Journey through the frozen land

Chapter Nine
Spirits of Nature

In the summer of 1925 Aleister Crowley travelled to Thuringen to meet the chiefs of various lodges in conference. With his characteristic humility, Uncle Aleister introduced himself as 'Sir Aleister Crowley' which must have impressed those title-hungry ritualists no end.

In the *Blätter für angewandte okkulte lebenskunst*, the newsletter of the Fraternitas Saturni, this conference is mentioned repeatedly. One fine day, we are told, Sir Aleister and his hosts went for a long walk up the garden path and into the forest. Whenever Uncle Aleister noticed a remarkable plant, stone or tree, he graciously lifted his hat to greet it. This bizarre behaviour apparently astonished his fellows. Some novices, we are told, dared to whisper 'What is the master doing?' 'The elemental spirits of nature have come to see the master' was the reply 'and Sir Aleister is acknowledging their greeting!' One of the group, Master Recnartus, head of Pansophia Lodge, asked Sir Aleister how he might invoke and see such an elemental spirit. The instructions were published by Gregor A. Gregorius, head of the Fraternitas Saturni, in an article on pentagram magick.

The magus is required to scratch this symbol at eye level with his magical dagger or knife into a lone or very ancient tree in some desolate place. One should imagine that the magical drawing of the pentagram symbol acts like a call that radiates some seven kilometres in all directions. Its radiance, fully charged by the will of an initiated magus, will be noticed by all in-between beings of the neighbourhood. It should be scratched under strongest concentration of desire and imagination. Useful is the hour of twilight at full moon or during the first phase of the waxing moon. Before departure, the master Magus ought to erase the calling sign while voicing thanks to the in-between beings.

Fraternitas Saturni gossip says that the above procedure does not necessarily function straight away. The novice is asked to try it at least 7 x 7 = 49 evenings, and if it doesn't work by then, to try another tree.

I hope that some of the more daring among you will now voice that obvious question 'Really, what is a nature spirit?' Frankly, I don't know. I have no idea what a spirit really is, or what I or you really are, let alone what reality may be. Luckily, we don't have to know. Do we require objective proof that some person really exists before we dare to mumble those sacred words 'Brother, would you lend me some cash?' Of course there are plenty of explanations as to just what the spirits may really be.

One model popular in Northern Europe claims that the spirits of nature are an expression of the life-force. In the old days of nature worship and head-hunting, the people believed that the spirits were everywhere. There were spirits in the plants and trees, for instance, who helped growth and gave individuality to each herb, plant, flower or tree. Especially the old and bizarre trees attracted the attention of the country people. 'Look at this tree' they would say 'there are faces in the bark! Maybe the spirit is showing itself!' The same sort of thinking was applied to the rest of the scenery. Great rocks were certain to house old rock-spirits, and while we're at it, we may as well mention river spirits, lake spirits, swamp spirits, well spirits, corn spirits, field spirits, flower spirits, animal spirits, hill spirits, mountain spirits, wind spirits, star spirits, rain spirits, sun spirits, moon spirits, helping spirits, house spirits and familiar spirits which makes the word 'spirit' an awfully vague term. Clearly, our ancestors lived in a world full of magical beings. Some of these spirits were considered friendly. Some elves, who live in flowers and herbs, were often friendly enough to reveal what medical use could be made of their plants. Closer to humans were the house spirits, the goblins or Kobolde, who require just a few morsels of good food to keep them happy and cheerful, and who will in turn protect the house and all who indwell it. Then there were the spirits of the places of power, who were guardians and initiators to the mysteries of long-forgotten cults, and the spirits of the wild forces of nature. Some of those nature spirits were fairly dangerous. A good many spirits of river, swamp and mountain demanded an annual sacrifice of man or beast. Should this ceremony be neglected, the angry spirit showed its wrath in tempests, floods or avalanches.

In the philosophy of the Greeks, starting with Empedocles (c.500-430 BCE), the world was considered as a blend of the four elements earth, water, fire and air. Quite naturally these elements had their spirits. Earth spirits were known as dwarves, gnomes, earth people and sometimes as giants. These beings were said to be the sentience of the earth, the consciousness of heavy, strong, formed and fertile matter. Some even considered the quartz crystals to be dwarves; the word 'quartz' comes from querch, which is a form of 'zwerch' or 'zwerg' meaning 'dwarf'.

The water spirits were called undines. These beings were thought to be larger and more graceful than the earth spirits, with beautiful bodies and lascivious minds. Like their element, the water spirits are ever in motion. Fire spirits or salamanders were known to live in earthquakes, lightning, volcanoes, sparks and flames. Usually these beings behave in wild and unpredictable ways. Lastly there were the wind spirits who had little form, but could see and hear and feel everything, and sing it out in endless songs. In the magical renaissance of the fifteenth century, the air spirits were often called 'the sylphs', which means 'forest spirits'.

This makes a lot of sense when we consider the role of the forest in the production of fresh air.

Often enough, the spirits were seen in a humanoid shape. The dwarves were believed to be tiny people living deep underground in the caves and hollows, dutiful labourers hard at work making crystals or telling the seeds which way to grow. Undines of either sex were known to spend long hours doing their hair or completing their makeup, from time to time they went to human festivities to drink, dance, and lure some love-struck lad or lass into a watery grave. Many folk tales describe how humans married water spirits, which usually didn't work out. Fire spirits were also humanoid, but tended to change their bright and radiant shape so fast that one could never really see them. The sylphs, on the other hand, could look just like trees if they chose. These spirits, as Paracelsus and others tell us, are shy and hide when humans are present. Though they have a friendly nature they will rarely speak in human words. Sometimes one sees them as moving: shadows between trees, seen out of the corner of the eye. Other sorts of wind spirits were known to shape the clouds or could be seen racing and howling with wild Wode (a local form of Wodan) on the storm wind.

In most of the old theories of the spirit world, people assumed that the spirits are actual entities, souls of the rocks, the plants, the forces of nature. Another interesting interpretation claims that the reality we perceive is of our own making. In this case, the spirits which we see in the trees are reflections of our own minds, and specifically reflections of those parts of our minds which are symbolized as 'tree consciousness'. If you would evoke, say, the spirit of a willow, you would effectively contact parts of your deep mind which respond to the willow symbol and feel familiar with such notions as 'water, sparkle, swaying, graceful curves, bending branches etc.'

The evocation of a rock spirit might reveal a lot about those parts of yourself that allow you to rest, to wait, to be patient while the evocation of the spirit of a mountain or forest might bring you in touch with a group consciousness, the sentience of the entire biosphere.

Another possible interpretation claims that some spirits, such as the guardian spirits, totem animals, allies or your personal deities, are mainly expressions of various parts of your deep mind, while the nature spirits, who live in plants and stone and greenery, have an existence independent of you. These beings, just like our personal gods and totems, are perceived by our minds, meaning that the shape we perceive them in is of our own making. Naturally this makes it very difficult to decide whether a given spirit is part of us or part of the local ecosystem. In practice, we don't have to decide. Much more important is the question of what the contact with some spirit does for you? Do you learn anything new? Do you find balance, healing, become whole in the process? Do you enjoy the contact? Does it inspire you?

One useful magical model will be outlined next. It is the shamanic theory which views the ecosystem as a single, living entity composed of myriads of different life forms, all of which depend on each other. Over the last decades, biology began to discover that living beings cannot be seen outside of the context in which they exist, and that in each and every ecological system all participants are connected with each other. In this sense we may consider a biosphere as a single living entity and the hypothesis that the biosphere of this planet is also a single, living entity, is but an extension of this idea. This idea is by no means new. We encounter it in most 'primitive' societies, in most shamanic theologies, in the Maatian 'N'aton' gestalt and in the 'Gaia hypothesis'.

If the world is a living being we are as much part of it as are the beasts, the plants, the fungi, trees and stones. Whichever life form we encounter can be seen as an extension of ourselves (and vice versa), aspects of a vast, multi-personal self that includes all participants in a single Gestalt. This makes all living beings close relations, and considering the DNA coding, this claim is not religion but biology. Thus, the interaction of one life form with another can be understood as communication of self with self. In this vast agglomeration, the all-self, each life form seems to fulfil a valid function. Each is specialized to do a specific job, both for itself and the biosphere, and the health of the whole depends on the balanced cooperation of all entities.

In the shamanic word view (I use the term 'shaman' to specify an international phenomenon, not the north Siberian sorcery tradition which coined the term), the mind is organized, much like the ecosystem. Indeed, it is often believed that the mind and the ecosystem reflect each other, and influence each other, as is the case when the community gathers to pray and dance to make rain. In the beginning of this book I often spoke of 'parts of the mind', which is a metaphor that modern people find easier to digest than such notions as 'gods', 'spirits' or whatever. Do you remember how those 'parts of your mind' do their work, how each of them is specialized to fulfil a special function, and how they are harmonized by the mutual, or 'true will'?

In the shamanic model, the 'parts of the mind' appear in natural shapes. They are organized and symbolized by shapes of nature, so that they appear as the 'spirits' or 'gods' of beasts, plants, trees, fungi, crystals, rocks, scenery, rivers, lakes, oceans, mountains, forest, desert, wind, air, clouds, lightning, rain, snow, ice, sun, moon, stars, plus an assortment of humanoid figures, such as the ancestors, the guardians, the ancestral shamans and some impossible beasts such as dragons, unicorns or crystal spiders. In this model, the 'spirit of a beast' would refer to some active and dynamic part of the deep mind, the 'spirit of a tree' would be more passive, while a rock spirit might be so simple, solid and enduring that you won't find words to express its meaning to your mind.

To the shaman the natural world (outside) and the mental world (inside) are closely connected. They are organized in similar ways, they include the same items, and they can influence each other. A crow croaking in the late afternoon, sitting on an oak, then taking to wing and flying north—this gesture would be very specific information to our shaman, as crows, croaks, oaks, late afternoons and north are all very meaningful in his/her reality, and make sense as specific symbols for specific parts of the deep mind. When the outside world is considered a reflection of the deep mind, life will be full of messages and secret meanings. Did you try the rites of mandala building? You connected the items of the outside world (the plants) with an assortment of meanings they have for your mind. The ritual created a link. The plants you worked with won't be simple plants any more: if you see one of them today, it will contain a lot of meaning for you.

To the shaman, witch or healer, the world is full of such meaningful plants. After some years of practice, all nature will mean something special to you. When a given plant, beast or stone carries a meaning it can become a message. Through the medium of nature, speaking the language and symbolism of life, the 'great spirit', the mutual sentience of the all-self can reveal itself. This is what a shaman means when s/he says 'well the crow and the oak told me this and that.' Quite possibly neither the crow nor the oak were aware that they triggered a message in our shaman, but as long as this message is valid, the system seems to work well. In some trances, the shamans identify their environment so closely with their minds that they are in effect travelling through their minds. This can be a wonderful experience when one is out in the forest. In a modern city, things can be pretty awful. Could a super market be a reflection of your mind? Let us dissociate the supermarket; the mind it reflects belongs to some other fool.

Enough of the models to contact the nature spirits, I would like to propose some experiments in creative hallucination. Our first exercise is to hallucinate human meaning into natural shapes. Many of us did this during childhood, when we discovered that this rock 'has a face' or that tree 'looks at me in such a sinister way'.

Exercise four: creative hallucination

Go out into nature, be it the country, a forest, the seaside or some public park or cemetery. Give yourself time to relax and to tune in to the natural world. If you like, you can induce a nice and pleasant trance to make you more aware of all the life around. Select some stone or tree that looks impressive and catches your attention through its unique appearance. What does this sight mean to you? If this rock or tree were part of your deep mind, what would its function be? The trick is to

Spirit Wood

identify with the stone or tree. How can you do it? As usual, I don't know. You do, however. That is, your deep mind knows, and if you experiment a little, will reveal just what turns you on.

Let us assume you have found a large stone. First you'll need to contact, see it, feel it, hear it, sense it as intensely as you can. Give yourself a lot of time. Describe what you sense, and as rocks are rather slow, allow yourself to slow down. How would this stone feel? Does it rest or does it stand? Does it lie, or sit, or squat, or lurk, or crouch, or sleep, or dream? Is the stone awake? Do you think the stone perceives you? What sort of meaning would you attribute to it? What would it be like if you were that stone? Can you imagine being in this place, day after day, year after year, in rain and snow and sunshine?

Sometimes when I walk the woods in trance, I go very much into the sense of seeing. At such times, much of the inner monologue fades or is simply forgotten, while I stare wide-eyed and void-minded. Then I move my eyes so that they touch and make contact. Seeing a tree, I see the bark and feel it with my eyes, the texture and the mosses on the surface, the pressure in the wood, the angle of the twigs, the motions of the branches as they grow, the lightness and flexibility of the foliage dancing in the wind. Seeing, I can feel the warm sunspots on the stem, the density of the roots as they clutch the soil, the swaying of the branches. Each of these sights is perceived as feeling.

Can you move your eyes over a tree, feeling the form, feeling the growth and meaning of the form? If your arms were branches, or if the tree's branches were arms, what would each gesture mean to you? What about the posture of the tree? Does it stand upright or does it lean, or bend, or twist, or dance? Can you assume this posture with your body? Can you name its meaning in human words?

What we have done in these exercises is to hallucinate human meanings into essentially non-human phenomena. Of course we don't know whether some tree with an upright shape really feels 'proud', all we know is that this sort of posture would mean 'proudness' in ourselves. We cannot know whether our hallucinations have anything to do with the consciousness of that tree, just as we cannot assume to know what the gestures of other people mean to them. And yet we all do that, more often than we realize. Can you remember seeing your lover with, say, a tense face, or a compressed mouth? And isn't it easy to hallucinate that this means 'anger' or 'frustration' or, worse? It's pure hallucination to assume that one knows what such symptoms mean to another. True, you may guess, and sometimes you may guess moderately well, but all in all you can never be sure. The muscular tension could mean dozens of things you never bothered to guess or think about. And yet, how often did you receive such signals, leap to some conclusion, and insist on reacting by being upset, or hurt, or unhappy? When we try to sense the mood of a tree, we do not sense what this tree really experiences, but what we imagine it to experience. It is the effect of that tree on our minds that concerns us. If we view it as a symbol or a message, we will be aware that this message has an effect on us.

Try the following. Find some trees that look 'sad', 'gloomy' or 'unhappy' to you, this being the emotion that your mind receives out of the tree shapes. Now spend some time there. Does it influence your mood, your state of mind? Then try the other extreme. Find some 'enchanted trees' or trees that look 'powerful' and 'magical'. What is it like to be there? It doesn't really matter whether the trees feel this enchantment. As long as you receive that message, and react to it, the enchantment may be quite subjective and nevertheless it will be real enough for you.

Do you remember what the trees were like when you were a child? Can you remember discovering strange faces and bizarre figures in their growth? Can you see (or imagine) beings, places, landscapes in the folds and lichens of a rock? Do you remember your childhood? What it was like going to bed? When the light was turned off could you see creatures lurking in the gloom?

Here we come to an exercise which Leonardo da Vinci made popular among the crazier sort of artist. A friend of his lived in a town that had a spitting wall. This was an ordinary old and rotten brick wall full of cracks, coloured spots and holes. The wall was dedicated to some saint. People believed that it was good luck to spit against the wall in passing. One day Leonardo's painter friend passed the wall and was struck by all the amazing visions, the bizarre scenes and fantastic entities he could observe in the colours, cracks, and ancient slime layers. Apparently, he spent hours staring wide-eyed at this wall. Then he hurried to tell Leonardo of his experience, who speedily passed the practice to like-minded associates. As not all painters are lucky enough to have such a ghastly wall in their neighbourhood, or feel too lazy to build and decorate one, Leonardo advised cloud-gazing as a simple alternative. This lofty occupation has the advantage that it can be practised in a relaxed posture, which may well ease the natural onset of trance or half-sleep.

A similar and well-known phenomenon is the Rorschach test. It seems that when we confront the mind with random shapes of sufficient complexity, the mind will attempt to see the available material in meaningful forms. Perhaps you would like to try this out. Select some highly complex structure, such as great clouds or coarse rocks, and relax. Go into a light trance if you like. Look at the forms. Watch the surface. Stare at it without naming the details.

Can you see without speech? There are many ways of stopping the inner monologue. We don't have to be drastic to effect this. Sometimes it's enough to allow the inner voice to fade for a while, or to forget it, or to be too busy seeing to give attention to the words. If you have to have an inner voice running, you might ask it to change the program. As long as you tell yourself that this is just rock with some cracks here and an edge over there and a couple of colour spots and the greenish stuff is just moss your mind will stick to the interpretation you are voicing. It's a reasonable interpretation and a restrictive one, if what we want to do is to imagine new forms into the given materials. Sometimes I bypass the 'reasonable inner voice' by making it an unreasonable one. Can you speak in chaos language to yourself?

Can you hear your inner voice making music or singing abstract sound patterns? Can you listen to the absence of sound? This may be simple and difficult at once. Just look at your rock surface. Imagine you don't know what it is, you are simply seeing form. If you do that for long enough, no doubt all sorts of figures and shapes will appear. Maybe it will be difficult at first. It's a skill that can be developed.

What is happening? Where did this rock get its face from, a fantastic face that appeared for a moment and then disappeared into the normal shapes of an ordinary rock surface again? Personally, I suspect that rocks (and anything else) are much more complex and wonderful than we usually realize. When one hemisphere of the brain stops naming this wonderful phenomena an 'ordinary rock' and shuts up for a moment, the other hemisphere may get a chance to sense this rock as unique and new experience, and to experience it as something new and original.

Given enough random structures, the mind is free to hallucinate all sorts of fascinating dream figures. This is one of the ways that ancient seers and prophets found wisdom and insight by staring into incense smoke or a burning bush if they came upon one. The same sort of thing happened to Odin hanging on a tree. After days of fasting and exhaustion, our 'ancestral shaman' god found the random shapes of the branches to align themselves in meaningful geometric patterns, and received the runes out of them.

Exhaustion and inner silence are simply two ways to get the imagination going. Fear is another. Carlos Castaneda frequently describes how Don Juan scares him with allies, night creatures, monster spirits and evil-minded sorcerers. As soon as Castaneda gets thoroughly terrified, he finds them lurking everywhere and the resulting fear tends to make the vision stronger. As this is one of the best acts in his program, he repeats the fear-routine in every volume. What would this method be good for? Nothing like a little fear to upset an ego that tries to be too reasonable.

Now for the actual evocation of the nature spirits. You have read how Crowley supplied a sigil, and this sigil tells us a lot about the process. The 'upside down' pentagram is supposed to call the spirits. Its base bears a symbol of earth, as the desired spirits are those of nature. Its four tips, which are usually assigned to the four elements, show a moon sickle each, which indicates that the spirits of the four elements should appear in the astral or lunar realm of dream, reflection and imagination. The shape in the middle may perhaps suggest a beetle, which connects it with the Tarot Atu 'The Moon', a card that has a lot to do with the realms of dream and hallucinations.

For a start, I would like to point out that we will 'see' our nature spirit with the 'eyes of the imagination', meaning that the vision will be much like a vivid daydream. We will watch a very subjective sight, as our spirit will assume a form that suits our understanding. It is not unusual that two people to receive two widely different visions of the same spirit, both of them being right. Your vision will not be quite the same as that of anybody else. This is quite natural. The information you receive will be processed and represented by your mind, and as your mind is unique, so will be your vision. Far too many budding mages frustrate themselves trying to have the same visions that the authorities describe.

Remember all the curious visions that Castaneda describes? How many of you have tried to see 'holes in the aura', or the motions of the 'assemblage point'? Did you take these ideas as facts or as metaphors? In all visions we are dealing with two basic items: a form which we perceive, and a meaning which this form has for us. Forms have different meanings to different people. When our deep mind wants to communicate with us, it will have to use a form that suggests the right meaning to us. These forms can be very different, even if their meaning is the same. Now as it happens, most of you won't be Mexican intellectuals with a split-personality. If the visions you receive are exactly like those of Castaneda (or of me, or anybody else) you are probably fooling yourself. Can you dare to be original?

What do we need to see a tree spirit? First of all, we obviously require a tree. If you choose a strong and healthy tree this is a good start; diseased or crippled trees can lead into difficult visions. The same goes for trees which stand too close to traffic or industry; such trees are not likely to have a good opinion of people. The ideal tree for our experiment is one which you have known and loved for years. Such a tree could well house a spirit who feels sympathy for you.

Next, consider the season. I find it easier to contact tree spirits during spring, summer and autumn when the tree is active and the sap

Seed Elves

flows, than in winter when much of its awareness rests in the roots. This does not go for evergreens, who can be evoked anytime during the year, and for some very special trees who might be considered good friends. Such trees will recognize you even when they sleep and dream. Make sure that you are well acquainted with your tree. The 7 x 7 repetitions of Crowley's formula do just that: even the most city-bound mage will begin to consider a tree as a living being after spending fortynine evenings with it.

From now on my technical advice will become somewhat vague. I can tell you some of the methods which may increase your chances, and can provide a framework of conditions which will make the evocation easier for you. In the actual working you are on your own. Feel free to use any method that suits you. If you have practised some of the techniques given in this volume, your chance of success will be pretty good. If you have learned to invent your own techniques, and apply the described techniques in creative and unusual ways, you are in a much better position. This book wasn't written to produce some new tradition of exercises and technical skills. Real magick is not merely an assortment of skills and techniques. It's more like an open minded attitude, a blend of interest and dedication, which allows each honest mage to observe, to learn, to adapt, and to invent unique new ways of changing identity and reality from within. Are you willing to learn from yourself?

The actual job of seeing a tree spirit is both simple and difficult. Speaking with the tree is a sound practice, as it will amplify your experience and bring you closer in touch with it. Perhaps the tree spirit won't understand your words. It is certain to understand your mood and attitude. A feeling of genuine sympathy is the best possible link. In a sense this rite is as much an act of love as all evocation is: one comes to communicate with an aspect of the universe one was previously unconscious of, and this act of communication is an act of union.

Embrace your tree and speak with it. Allow yourself to slow down, relax and drift into a gentle trance state. Call into the tree, tell it that you will to see its spirit, ask it in a friendly way to show itself in a shape you can understand. Lean your head against the tree. Look at the bark, feel how you embrace the stem, allow your eyes to close. Imagine that you are seeing the bark, just as you saw it when your eyes were still open. If your imagination isn't vivid enough, open your eyes briefly and have another look. Repeat this until you can 'see' the bark with closed eyes. Then imagine that the bark becomes transparent and that you can look into the tree, which may appear much like a hollow tube. Look into your tree. Can you see the roots, can you see the branches? Some people see the spirit straight away. Some see it, but do not recognize it, as is usually the case when ego insists that this or that phenomenon ought to fulfil its expectations.

As ego frequently expects the wrong sort of event, or focuses attention in some unprofitable direction, it is quite possible that we spend a lot of time waiting for something which is already happening, though in a form we do not recognize. Some see the spirit in a humanoid form. Some perceive it in hearing, or feeling, before an image appears. Some receive a wealth of tree wisdom, and then complain they haven't seen the spirit at all. *Whenever your ego expects something specific, you are certain to miss something vital.* The spirit of the tree will not behave as you expect it to. It may reveal itself in one form or in a hundred, it may be moody, or friendly, or angry. It may deceive you, or play with you, send you all sorts of strange insights or pretend it isn't there at all.

Don't worry. Given enough patience, you'll get used to it. Some people are anything but patient. They receive a little bit of something or other during the first attempt, then make a great scene trying to evaluate, to analyse, or worse yet, trying to find out if they did it right. How do they do that? They ask their ego whether the experience accords with expectations, which, quite naturally, it doesn't. Oh, dear! The next step is to worry, to fall into doubt, to demand instant results, to feel incompetent and to declare the entire event a 'failure'. Often enough ego begins to howl 'I can't do it!!!' Which is true, and natural. It's not the conscious mind which works the vision, nor is it the conscious mind which contacts the spirit or represents its form and meaning. All of these are worked by the deep mind, which works much better when ego shuts up and stops meddling.

How often does it happen that people master new skills during the very first attempts? In magick, especially with invocation and evocation, we are discovering and integrating parts of ourselves which have been latent and unknown for most of our lives. It can take months and years to come to terms with them. Those who hurry too much will never make it.

Some people get good results seeing through the transparent bark of the tree. Some require a long and detailed invocation, prayer or call. Others are more passive, and contact the tree spirit by waiting. Then there are those who like to imagine that they walk into the tree, and travel up and down the stem until they encounter some being. Another good variation is to transform into a tree, a little bit of shape-changing already described in *Helrunar*. Here is a outline of the technique:

Exercise five: shape shifting

Find some open space close to the trees you wish to contact. Stand with your feet together, the hands hanging at your sides. Take a couple of deep breaths, then relax and close your eyes. Quite leisurely, you will now imagine that you become a tree. Can you feel your body as a pillar. . . as a single line. . . a solid stem. . . of layer upon layer. . . of strong wood. . . can you see the bark. . . that covers your skin. . . and hides your face. . . surrounding the core. . . of your being. . . so that you rest. . . deep within. . . the silence. . . feeling good. . . within yourself. . . move your attention. . . can you sense your feet. . . as they touch the ground. . . and feel that the roots grow out of your feet. . . long roots. . . tough roots. . . strong roots. . . that reach deep. . . deep down. . . down into the soil. . . into the earth. . . and through the humus. . . into the deeper realms. . . through pebbles and stones. . . into the deep. . . and deeper still. . . clinging to solid rock. . . firmly anchored. . . drinking the rich dark waters. . . that flow deep below the surface and you can sense the sap as it rises. . . as it moves. . . and transports all the nourishment of the deep upwards. . . Can you feel how the stem transports the juices and

Ghosts of the Beech Grove

that you slowly begin to sway as the tree sways and attention moves to the height... to the branches... as they out fold... out of you shoulders. .. out of your head... the branches grow... Feel them grow... Reaching out... reaching up... Firm branches... elastic twigs and lush foliage. .. Leaves that bend and dance and sway in the breath of the wind... The tree swaying under the wide sky... in the cycles of nature... there is life in the land... There is joy in being alive.

Adapt this basic pattern to suit your needs and desires. Once you have become sufficiently like a tree, you can learn a lot of things about trees, nature and earth you were hitherto unconscious of. A very similar practice was developed by Albert Einstein, whom some consider a serious and respectable 'objective' scientist. Einstein, showing great initiative, dared to be subjective. One of his 'gedanken-experimente' was to spend long hours imagining that he was a photon flying through space. What sort of life would a photon lead? I don't know, and probably Einstein didn't know either. His imagination was quite subjective, after all. And yet it led him to discover all sorts of unusual things about space and time that more 'objective' scientists wouldn't have dared to dream of.

What about the other spirits in nature? The essential patterns used to evoke a tree-spirit can easily be adapted to the spirits of plants, herbs, worts and flowers. Stone spirits can be difficult. If you are calm and patient, and give yourself a lot of time, you can tune in to stone consciousness. Some stones are full of surprises. There are esoteric teachings which claim that stones, particularly if they are rich in quartz, will collect and conserve strong thoughts and feelings. A rock which has been involved in strong magical outbursts of ceremony and passionate emotion will retain this information for years, if not for centuries. Rocks have been charged with vivid ideas to create natural temple spaces. This information, hidden in many rocks in many sacred sites or sanctuaries, has its own 'wavelength'. Most of the tourists that crawl all over the place won't even notice it. Those with talent for magick can perhaps tap a couple of those memories which are related to them. Those who work patiently and bother to explore a rock for months or years, may find that many cults of different ages worked their magick nearby, and that each of them left a different memory stream tuned to some wavelength in the stone.

In practice, its useful to spend a lot of time with the rock of your choice. Leaning your head against it, you can allow your eyes to close and imagine you are seeing into it. A similar practice is mentioned by Frater Achad in a paper on clairvoyance. As Achad mentions, it can sometimes be too much of a strain to stare at or into a crystal ball. As trance sets in, and the sight of your crystal blurs, it can happen that the eyes feel tired and wish to close. This is quite acceptable. You can continue looking into your crystal with closed eyes, and forget about the crystal when the visions begin.

Then there are those who practice psychometry, and attempt to look into the past of a given object using the imagination. Usually the object is held for a while, and is then placed on the brow or the solar-plexus. With closed eyes our medium looks into the object, keeping a very open mind, ready to receive all sorts of sensations. Some look into the object as if it were transparent. Others imagine the object is covered with a veil or curtain, and open it when they are ready. More daring adventurers imagine the object is open, and walk into it, and into the strange worlds beyond. Some objects have known so much magical use that they can actually initiate an open-minded seer. Others have a wild and bloody history, which can have one hell of an effect if the seer doesn't dissociate swiftly enough.

What value do our visions have? We cannot expect to perceive objective realities using our subjective minds. It would be pretty stupid to insist that any vision is 'true' or 'real', no matter how vividly it is perceived. We don't have to believe or disbelieve what we experience. Ultimately, the sole test of quality is what you make out of it. If a vision touches you, moves you, teaches, inspires or transforms you, this vision, no matter whether it is 'true' or 'illusionary', is genuine enough.

What about the elemental spirits? How about exposing yourself to the elements? Far too many modern witches work in the comfort of their well-heated living rooms, thinking abstract little thoughts about this symbol and that metaphor, and never bothering to recognize the raw wild force that abides in every element. Fire and water, wind and earth, have become mere symbols to the city-dwellers. To our ancestors, they were reality, meaning that sheer survival depended on them. How much fire will you discover in your nature when most of the fires you have seen happened to burn on television? How can you trust the healing powers of the earth when most of the earth you know happens to be covered with asphalt and concrete? Would the undines appreciate being contacted through a glass of tap-water? Of course there are people who can do that, who can evoke fire spirits from candles or earth spirits from flowerpots. When you have experienced the elemental spirits out in nature, where they are active and strong, and have come to enjoy sunshine and rain showers, wild winds, cross-country walks and snowstorms, you will know them well enough to contact them everywhere.

To evoke an elemental spirit you would do well to expose yourself to that element. The earth spirits in open country, where you can touch and smell and taste the soil, show a marked difference to the earth spirits of the city. From an abstract point of view one might argue that earth, as it symbolizes the abstract principles of form, weight, solidity and endurance, is present in city and country alike. These qualities, however, are certainly not all there is to earth. Some of us, thank goddess, have an innate interest in the life-giving virtues of earth, and these, as practice shows, are anything but manifest deep in the concrete grandeur of our man-made environments. It's easier to understand the elements in their natural form. When you sit by the side of a stream hearing the water gurgle and sing, feeling its cool moistness, watching the sparkle of light, the rhythm of the waves, the dance of bubbles and foam, you will stand a very good chance of recognizing the essence of water, be it in nature, be it as the spirit of that stream, or within your own nature. In the right mood and environment the contact can take place quite naturally.

In practice, you will notice that contact to some spirits is easier than to others. If you are of a wild and lusty temperament, the fire spirits will be more in accord with your nature than the slow and patient spirits of the earth. In this case, a fire working will be easy, but an earth working will be twice as valuable, as it will give you a chance to develop new aspects and talents of yourself. To the professional magus, each new spirit, god or entity represents a chance to discover and develop a new self-aspect. Let us remember congruence. If you desire to meet fire spirits, you would do well to light a large fire. To be congruent with this fire you could dance around it, screaming and chanting till exhilaration grips you and sweat runs all over your skin. When you have become very fiery, make contact. Close your eyes. See the flames in your imagination. Call to the fire spirits to appear. Then imagine you walk straight into the fire, into a world composed of heat, light, brightness and intensity. The beings you may meet in the dancing flames will really know fire, as it is their pure essence, substance, consciousness and form. As you come to terms with them, you will equally come to terms with the fire aspects in your own nature.

How can you be congruent with the other elements? Earth spirits can be reached in a state of rest and deep relaxation. Water spirits correspond to our dreamy and emotional nature, and consequently you may find it easy to meet them in a state of gentle drowsiness, with body swaying softly, speech surging and pulsing, like the rhythm of the waves. Air spirits are more subtle. Exposure to wind helps, as does prayer, singing, dancing, deep breaths, free speech and an open sky. Don't expect them to be as solid, dynamic or well defined as the others: it's in their nature to be fleeting and fast. Each of the spirits is a specialist. Each of them knows very much of its own element, and very little of the others. It logically follows that if we want a balanced concept of the whole, we will have to meet as many different specialists as we can. To focus extensively on one single sort of spirits or gods can seriously upset the balance. Thus, when we leave the world of an element, we do well to release the energy-excess into its source, remembering that healing requires the living wholeness of ourselves.

Earthing

How can we release an energy-excess? If you feel 'over loaded' or 'upset' after contact to a tree spirit, you could simply release the excess into the tree. As you touch your tree, saying 'Thank you!' to its spirit, allow the energy to rush out of you and back into its proper abode. Imagine the energy vividly. There should be a definite physical sensation of 'outflow', telling you that you are doing fine. Another simple gesture is to stretch. Lift your hands as high as possible, now, giving a mighty howl, drop to the ground. As you lie on the earth, imagine that the excess-energy rushes out of your body and into the nameless depths below. Breath after breath, you release the force into the earth. Give yourself time and allow yourself to relax.

This sort of 'earthing' should be involved in most rituals. It gives solidity to the working, allowing all the evoked forces to find shape and flesh and form by manifestation on earth. Think of all the good things that will manifest out of the power, once it has rushed out of you into the earth to find manifestation in the world of reality. It is a sign of the advanced mage to lay a lot of emphasis on earthing. To avoid earthing is to become bloated with unbalanced energies: to hoard power is an excellent way of making it stagnate and putrefy. At the end of the rite we release the excess-energy into the ground. This power is not lost. There is consciousness in it, the sentience of our working, and this 'child', which is both energy and intelligence, will begin to live once we let go of it.

Spirits of Wind and Air

Chapter Ten
Waking the Beasts

Here is a chapter dedicated to the joys of working magick with the beast spirits. Before we can plunge into the practice, however, I would like to summarize and develop a few theoretical points. Quite possibly you may have found the theories implied by the last chapter difficult to comprehend, and this, alas, is how it should be. When we deal with such metaphors as 'gods', 'spirits', 'conscious' and 'subconscious minds' and the like, we are not describing reality as it is but as it can appear to us. When I speak of the structures of consciousness I am not describing any sort of reality but a series of magical and psychological models which may or may not be of use in coming to terms with the unknown. The efficiency of these models depends on how you use them. In some previous exercises, you have (hopefully) glimpsed or met some nature spirits. You may recall that difficult question—is a nature spirit an aspect of yourself or is it an independent entity? Adherents of a more psychological theory will probably prefer to consider the nature spirits as projections of their own minds.

Maggie/Nema proposes an alternative point of view: 'Consider this proposal: if all that is lives; all that lives is intelligent. We recognize esoterically several levels of life: animal, vegetable, protozoan, bacterial, viral. Would it not be possible for there to be mineral intelligence, thinking extremely slowly via crystal pressure-changes? Would it not be possible for there to be solar life, thinking by means of the plasma's convection currents? Would it not be possible for there to be subatomic life, thinking by means of the spins, charges, quantum band shifts and traversing the matter-energy distinction?'

Obviously we cannot decide whether a given nature spirit is a meaningful hallucination produced by our minds or has an independent life in the same sense as our next door neighbours. More so, the question, when framed of the 'either/or' basis, is simply too limited. Both explanations have their shortcomings. What do you think about a statement like this: 'Well, when I contact the fire spirits, I contact the ancient sentience of fire as it has always been and will ever be. I am also making contact with those aspects of myself which can be called fiery, such as the heat of metabolism, the energetic system and those parts of my mind which connect with power, heat, lust, wild instinct, motion and the like.'

How do you like this explanation? Would you like to live in a world that goes beyond rudimentary 'either/or' thinking, extending into the wealth of potential expressed as 'both/neither and maybe'? If evocation reveals anything, it is the fact that our very limits and self-descriptions are artificial. Essentially, your self, myself, all-self and no-self extend everywhere.

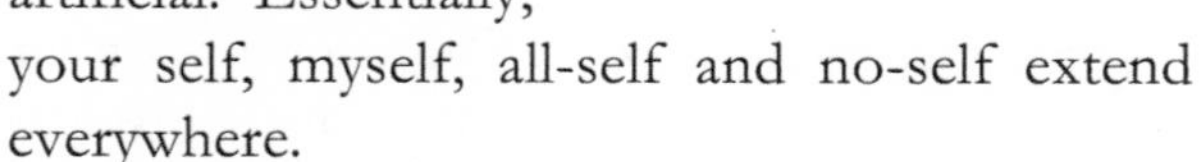

The model of the mind as an ecosystem has already been mentioned. Applying it, you would describe the various parts of your mind as 'spirits' which might appear in all sorts of shapes, such as stones, crystals, mushrooms, flowers, plants, trees, beasts, plus an assortment of natural atmospheric phenomena and various ancestors or imaginary entities. These shapes are representations of their functions, symbolic forms to facilitate easier comprehension. Often enough those shapes are seen in highly anthropomorphic guise, suited to the human trait of perceiving human meaning in essentially non-human phenomena. Dare we admit that our conscious minds are very simple creatures who prefer to think in terms of common things rather than abstract principles?

What can the spirits do? What can the parts of the mind do? There is a part of the mind, for instance, which tells you when to eat. When it realizes that the body's reserves are getting exhausted it produces a powerful signal which makes your conscious mind say 'Hey! I guess I must be hungry!' Now hunger is one of the strongest signals in our system. As it is connected so closely to some survival drives, it can be pretty hard for the conscious mind to ignore it. On the other hand, there is this useful feeling: 'Gods! I can't eat anymore!' Which signals quite definitely when we have had enough food. When this part does its job well, your system will get as much food as it requires. Should it do its job even better than that, it will manage to tell you exactly which sorts of food you are needing.

This, however, is a skill that has to be developed. Another part of the mind signals when you need rest or sleep. When this is the case, you will receive a signal that tells you 'to bed'. Mind you, the signal may differ from person to person. Some will recognize that they need sleep when they begin to feel slightly irritated. Others will require an hour of heavy yawning to recognize the same thing, and some will fall asleep simply to find out that they really need it.

The part that has the job 'make sure of sufficient sleep' knows the conscious mind it has to live with. Long experience has taught what signals that person will need to be motivated for bed. In our shamanic symbolism we might perceive the part that controls the feeding as a crocodile, a shark, a wolf, a bear or a wild boar, for example. The part that controls sleep might be some animal who hibernates, or perhaps a beast of the night, such as owl or bat, symbolizing the power of the dreamer to travel the dark. One of the interesting points in this model is that the parts of the mind are unique for each person. We all have learned to develop a part that says 'Hey! I'm hungry!' In its own subtle way, otherwise we wouldn't have lived to read this book. We might consider that 'hunger/feeding' is a function necessary for survival, and that each of us has found an efficient way to fulfil this function. Not all of us, however, have parts which function as well as they could. With some people hunger signals are not strong enough—which is quite typical for head-bound business people on a tough schedule—while others receive strong hunger signals resulting in all sorts of overeating. Using our shamanic symbolism, we might claim that some require a hungry crocodile in their bellies to get sufficient food, while others would be much happier with a small squirrel spirit who would move around a great deal while requiring only small portions of food.

How many magicians are aware of what they do with their bodies anyway? Now in our model, we have scores, if not hundreds of parts and sub-parts that work our behaviour for us. Many of them have learned to ensure that you get food, shelter, love, rest, security, friendship, joy, fresh experience, good health, motion and magick, to name just a few basic needs, and these parts have learned to do their job as well as they can. You may perhaps believe that you do most of these things automatically or by habit, but this is just another way of saying that it is not your conscious but your deep mind which has learned to do them for you.

All 'habits' were once consciously learned (think of learning to eat, learning to walk, learning to read), and once you had mastered them your deep mind took over and did them for you, by 'habit' as you choose to call it. Do you know how many different actions are required in the simple act of tying your shoes? Some parts of your mind do curious things with the hands, others keep you in balance and others still observe that all actions are done properly, and in the right order. Ask your parents how long it took you to learn the entire process. At first there were weeks and months of conscious effort, plus any amount of trial and error. Then the act became memory. Today you put on your shoes without even having to think about it.

Serpent Sensuality

What would happen if someone offered you a much better method to tie your shoelaces? Before it could work, you would have to unlearn the old habitual method. Then you might consciously learn the new process. If your deep mind likes it, you will soon enough do it habitually. This, basically, is how the magick transforms our lives.

When I say that there are 'parts of the mind' which do this and that for you, the label is meant as a convenience. Modern brain research, however, has clearly shown that there are, indeed, specialized parts of the brain which do specific things for the whole system. E. Rossi mentions an interesting one in his book *The Psychobiology of Mind-body Healing*:

> *The mind's ability to attend to the new has its psycho-biological basis in the activity of a cluster of norepinephrine-containing neurons in the* locus coeruleus *of the pons area of the brain stem. When novel stimuli are received by the* locus coeruleus*, its neural connections stimulate the onset of brief states of heightened responsiveness in the higher cortical areas of the brain, and in the limbic-hypothalamic centre that integrates memory and houses the reward or pleasure mechanisms. Dull, repetitive situations, on the other hand, decrease the activity of the* locus coeruleus *and lead to relaxation, drowsiness and sleep.*

Can you imagine how useful this part is when you want to recognize and learn something new? How new experiences can become a strong stimulant that heightens brain-activity and reward you with feelings of pleasure? How would you name and symbolize this part?

Many of the parts of our minds are busy with the basic survival needs. The part that regulates appetite is one of the oldest, as it began learning its job very shortly after birth. It did have to learn quite a few things since then and it learned them quite well, or some of us would still show the feeding behaviour of early infancy. With most people, these parts are not part of their conscious human personality. Nevertheless these parts are there, are elements of our genetic heritage, the DNA structure that evolved us into almost human beings.

We all have parts in our minds which know, genetically, how to use and apply aggressive behaviour, no matter whether our conscious minds can accept them or not. A good many of our ancestors (I am not just referring to some 60,000 years of homosapiens but to countless millions of animal life) had to be extremely aggressive, even 'amoral' by our standards to survive.

This sort of information is still existent in your DNA, just as are the countless aeons of life on a level that was too simple (or primitive) to know aggression at all. Veneration of the ancestors, as can be commonly found in Voodoo and Taoism, is not an abstract concept at all. If you want to meet your ancestors, few of whom were human, be welcome to meet them in every cell of your body. Every cell of your body contains the entire heritage of the evolution of our species. Much of this information is useless for modern life. A great deal of our present political problem stem from this, from the all-too-human tendency to use out-of-date methods for new problems.

We were speaking of aggression, which is a mode of problem-solving that has been highly efficient for millions of years of animal life. It is a curious thing that when we dare to recognize that we have aggressive parts in our mind's ecology, we will stand a good chance of leading a happy and peaceful life. Aggression can be useful. It can provide the power to overcome obstacles, to break down restrictions and to XYZ. (Please invent a couple of situations when solid aggression can help).

Aggression can also be a valuable signal. When I am getting worn out, tired, cramped, strained, or circumstances restrict and exhaust me, my aggression-level tells me how much more I can take. If you use aggression (or any other emotion) as a signal, you may realize that it means something when you find yourself snarling. You don't 'have aggression' in the same sense as people have cars, money or lice. Aggression is not an object one can own. You might ask yourself 'What are these aggressive feelings telling me?' and find out that maybe some part of your deep mind wants to protect you with them.

What do you do when you notice you are feeling aggressive? Do you enquire within what the feeling is telling you? Or do you simply proceed to hit someone? Or would you rather pretend the aggression doesn't exist? There are scores of ways of letting out aggression leading to all sorts of unpleasant side-effects. Wise people know that aggression, like any other strong emotion, is good for something. Wouldn't it be better to accept the signal for what it's worth, and to take the rest of the day off?

To remove the 'cause of aggression' is but part of the work. When body feels 'aggressive', this means that the brain has released a lot of neurotransmitters into your blood stream, most of which make 'fight or flee' an easier solution than 'wait and think!' Before you'll become peaceful again, you may have to deal with the chemicals that are making you so eager to hit something.

A good method to cope with an adrenaline overdose is to work it off, be it by running, dancing, a long country walk, singing and screaming wild music or the practice of a martial art of the more vicious variety. Most martial artists become fairly gentle people once their aggressive parts have learned that they can fight their way out every other day in the local Dojo. Compare this to the 'New-age think positive' types who try to transcend aggression by pretending it isn't there. Often enough they lose the ability of expressing any emotion at all. How many 'white-lighters' can be loud, wild, spontaneous, joyous or gladly mad? How good are your chances to heal a disease when you cannot honestly admit that it exists? Aggression is not a disease, it is merely a state of emotion which our ancestors found useful for various strategies of fighting, hierarchy and courtship behaviour. The 'disease' is what happens when people misapply the genetic inheritance, or try to repress it altogether.

Here we encounter the fact that the 'parts of the mind' will use any method which produces the desired result. Deep down, all human beings have a need for attention and affection. It's part of our inheritance. The apes who preceded us were social animals living in

small groups. A baby learns that it will get attention, and a measure of love, provided it screams long and loud enough. The infant has to learn that mere screaming will produce attention, but not necessarily love, and will have to develop a scope of alternative strategies. Later on, the child learns that attention can be gained by positive (socially acceptable) and negative methods. Biting, pinching and misbehaviour of your choice will produce attention, but fairly little love. Charm, interest, friendly gestures, skills and social behaviour are much more efficient to gain love. This insight has to be learned.

Children who misbehave are not necessarily 'evil', 'wrong' or 'stupid', often they are simply using the most basic strategy at their disposal to obtain the attention that they desire. Habit says that this strategy has worked before, and as they lack the freedom to choose a better method, they will use the old strategy, which, in spite of all its nasty side-effects, will certainly work.

We all have parts in our minds which help us to get the attention and the love we need. They do their job without our conscious recognition. There are plenty of people who would stoutly deny that they need love, let alone that parts of their nature work very hard at getting it.

The function—the need for love—is something we all share, but the actual behaviour we use to fulfil it differs enormously. Note that our baby, our infant, our child do not usually know that they want attention and love, at least not on the conscious level. Some people have developed hundreds of methods of getting love and the like, while others are still busy with the methods they should have outgrown at the age of five.

There are people who scream abuse at each other when they want love and affection. Usually they know that this is not exactly the best method, but then they usually don't know a better one. The part of their deep minds which wants to produce 'love' simply uses a method which will work. If it knew a better way, it would probably use it. As Grinder and Bandler emphasize in *Frogs Into Princes*, people are generally trying to make the best choice possible. If someone has to scream insults in order to win affection, this person simply has no better choice to fulfil a valid need.

All behaviour is learned. We all have certain needs. We all have methods to deal with these needs. Some of these methods will be good and others will be merely adequate, yet all these methods will work in their way. These methods are habitual. We know that they work as they have always worked. These methods constitute our behaviour, which, becoming regular and automatic, creates the illusion of a predictable, continuous, enduring personality. Even problematic behaviour, no matter how irrational it may seem, accords with the basic idea that it is useful for something. What do we do when we want to change our problematic behaviour? First of all we have to get in touch with the part of the mind which produces it by habit. Then we can find alternative methods of achieving our needs, strategies that produce the desired result using more efficient forms of behaviour. The works of Bandler and Grinder are well worth studying, especially *Frogs Into Princes*, *Trance Formations* and *Reframing* to get a good idea of how the sorcerous practice 'conjuring a spirit' can be improved.

So far, we have dealt with 'spirits' and 'parts of the mind'. As I don't want to reduce the miraculous in magick, here is another interpretation. When a simple minded Catholic wants to have a disease cured s/he does not consult a therapist (who believes in a part of the mind called the immune system) nor a shaman (who believes in healing spirits) but a Catholic saint who is known to be helpful with that specific disease. This saint would be contacted through prayer, emotion, imagination and sacrificial offerings, and if the rite is well done, the saint will work a 'miracle cure', which is the one reason anyone gives a damn for saints at all. Now Catholicism is really pantheism, in that it offers hundreds of saints, each of whom is specialized to work some very specific miracles. If you want a safe journey, you would get a talisman of St. Christopher, as can be seen in thousands of Italian cars. It's no use to approach St. Christopher when you want to win a card game, cure leprosy or mend a broken heart.

The same sort of thing can be observed in Tibetan Buddhism, where you get one central Buddha surrounded by thousands of minor Buddhas, Arhats, Avatars plus special variations. The same goes for Taoism. Though Tao may be all one, or none, and also nameless there is also its counterpart in ceremonial Taoism, which lists thousands of highly specialized spirits in a system too vast for comprehension. To deal with a specific problem, you can simply contact the specialist who is in charge.

In magick, we can learn a great deal by meeting all sorts of these specialists. Each spirit who is aligned in harmony and cooperation with the whole, corresponds with a self-aspect which is healed and made whole. In a sense we require both the monotheistic point on view, which states 'they are one' and emphasizes the unity of the system, and the pantheistic attitude which delights that 'they are many'. If you want a holistic effect, deal with the mind 'as one'. If you desire a specific effect, go to the specialist in charge. Both models are useful in their way. If we envision the parts of the mind as a lot of specialists doing their job, we may occasionally encounter problems if we don't know the proper specialist for a given task. At other times, it can happen that some of those specialists get too narrow minded and interfere with each other. Sometimes there may be friction, as is often the case when people feel themselves torn between choices. In such cases, it would be easiest to consult a class of spirits which might be called 'metaparts'; i.e. parts which coordinate the various specialists.

Have you ever wondered what the 'subconscious mind' may be? When you ask yourself 'Dear deep mind, would you allow me to remember my dreams?' who listens and who responds to the request? Who is this subconscious mind we are struggling to comprehend? To a good many people, the subconscious mind is something similar to Pandora's box: if you take off the lid, who knows what horrors may escape? Such people do not trust their deep minds, and by the same mouth their deep minds don't feel inclined to trust them. By definition, our subconscious minds consist mainly of those parts of our nature we are unaware of. Nobody knows what a subconscious mind really is—

and yet, when we use some metaphor to describe it, we will find that it responds and lives up to expectations. If you happen to be one of those poor sods who believe that the subconscious is a junkyard of neurotic impulses, repressed horrors, savage instincts and primitive survival drives (an attitude shared by a good many Freudian therapists) your subconscious mind will probably live up to your belief, and will produce all sorts of experiences to confirm it. If you should call your subconscious mind 'God', however, you will find yourself living in quite another world full of faith, divine blessing, enthusiasm and possibly miracles. Should you call it your 'inner genius', 'Daemon' or 'Holy Guardian Angel' you will enjoy its inspiration and help, and the expression of yourself in art, love, will and magick.

It seems that the subconscious mind, whatever it may be, behaves more or less as we expect it to. Don't ask me why, ask yourself. The deep mind of Dr. Freud, for instance, received positive feedback (i.e. pleasure) whenever it discovered some interesting new instinct, neurosis or taboo to keep the good doctor busy and content. As Freud delighted in the scientific study of neurosis, his deep mind kept him happy by producing more and more of it. Soon enough, Freud began to see neurosis everywhere—hardly surprising when we consider the society he had to live in—and as we all tend to emphasize what interests us, this must have made his reality a remarkably unpleasant dream to believe.

The deep mind of Dr. Jung received positive feedback whenever it recognized some interesting symbolism or mandala structure. It is no surprise that to Jung the world became a mysterious and fascinating alignment of archetypal patterns, and quite obviously, the world Jung made for himself was much more pleasant than the world of Freud.

By the same mouth, my deep mind has learned that it receives positive feedback whenever it reveals that the world changes under will, and consequently I enjoy living in a reality in which the worlds without and within interact, communicate and transform each other, as suits our nature and the circumstances.

We all do this sort of thing. Each of us has developed a deep mind which has learned to produce a specific reality for us, namely the reality the conscious mind expects and reinforces through the feedback of doubt, belief, pain, pleasure and so on. We all have learned to create a world through our beliefs, it is the world which we believe to be real. In this sense, each human being is a great magician. Each of us creates an entire world, and makes it so convincing that the illusion fools ourselves. We have learned to make a world, and then forgotten that its reality is of our making. We may remember.

Would you dare to believe in a better, changeable world full of unknown potential and pleasure? Would you dare to trust your many self-aspects, known and unknown, to transform and heal the whole of your being? Would you dare to discover the 'divine', the 'daemon', the 'spirit helpers', to address the deep, or subconscious mind? The answer is simple. I believe that behind all of these titles lies a mutual phenomenon which happens to be too vast for my comprehension. Each of the names, titles and metaphors is a road of access. You will (presumably) contact the same wonderful phenomenon, whatever title you use, but your contact will be specifically as you believe it. The rest is practice.

Beginners in magick usually do not enjoy speaking with their 'subconscious minds', as this entity is supposed to house all sorts of suppressed horrors. They will find it much easier to trust in 'the gods', and will find that the communion works miracles. The gods are, after all, part of a belief structure that allows miracles to happen. An atheist would be much happier believing and communing with the 'parts of the mind' or 'inner genius'. This belief structure will probably exclude 'miracles', but it has some advantages I'm too lazy to mention—do yourself a favour and think for yourself.

In Nepal, a young shaman is given a group of spirit helpers, who are magically sealed with food and fluids, inside of bamboo tubes. This gift is not an easy one. These spirits (they usually include the serpent, the wild boar, the silent dog and several others) are very wild and overwhelming at this stage: our young shaman has to learn how to live with them. During the first months, the spirits make plenty of trouble.

Sounding the Drum

As they are neither tame nor easy to control, all sorts of outbursts may take place. Often enough, s/he falls in and out of possessive trance, and has to struggle with all sorts of bestial urges. Obsession takes place, releasing any amount of raw energy and emotion. Gradually, the human and the bestial aspects of the mind come to know and appreciate each other. They begin to trust and transform each other, creating a solid foundation of magical cooperation. With growing familiarity, the spirits reveal themselves as friends and self-aspects. By this stage, the horrors of obsession become meaningless. What obsesses us in ritual is but another mask of self. Louis Martinie expressed it quite brilliantly in the *Cincinnati Journal of Magick*, Issue VII, 1989:

> *Possession by Loa, demons, angels, etc., is really not the issue. What most of us struggle with is possession by what is commonly known as Personality. To the extent that we identify with our personalities, we are possessed by those limiting definitions of self. Quite often what people fear most in ritual possession is a weakening of the hold of the personality on the self. It may be a small cage but it is at least familiar. Ritual possession is one way of breaking free from the confines of a too deeply entrenched personality.*

To the shaman, the gods and the spirits are friends. They come to aid the working, to join the fun of the festivities. The wild boar spirit, for example, is very skilled in detecting what lies hidden underground. When this spirit takes over and possesses the shaman, the latter will begin to scamper around on all fours, snorting and grunting, and searching the ground until the problem finally comes out. The serpent spirit is often at home in the tunnels and waterways of our systems. The shaman possessed by the serpent spirit will probably begin to hiss and sway. In this state, s/he can regulate the flow of fluids and energies, remove obstructions in the flow and suck out hidden poisons. Bird spirits are often good at divination. Possessed by a bird spirit, the shaman can take to wind and soar into the heights. Seen from a healthy distance, many human problems are easy to understand. The silent dog has a function akin to the Egyptian Anubis, or the Wolves of Wotan: travelling between the worlds. A shaman in silent dog consciousness can travel through the worlds of dream and imagination into realms inaccessible to human consciousness.

Usually, the shaman lives and works with several guardian spirits. In working magick s/he allows the spirits to arise and to take over. In a state of possession, the spirits act through the body of the shaman, revealing the unknown, doing the impossible, working the magick and the healing. In a psychological model, one might claim that the shaman has developed various parts of the subconscious mind to do various things (such as healing, magick, ritual, sorcery, etc.) which her/his conscious mind cannot do so well. In this context, the conscious mind is wise enough to step back and give control to these deep mind aspects, who consequently 'possess' the shaman's body to do their job. This would imply that the healing magick is aided by the shaman but performed and manifested by the gods and spirits of the system. This recalls Erickson's belief that the healing comes from the subconscious mind. 'The therapist is quite unimportant,' Erickson used to say, pointing out that the therapist's job is merely to create a climate, an atmosphere, in which healing takes place naturally.

The guardian spirits in shamanism function much like the 'metaparts' previously mentioned. Where the 'parts of the mind' fulfil functions and produce behaviour, the 'metaparts' coordinate them.

In the system of Abra-Melin the Mage, the chief coordinator is called the 'Holy Guardian Angel', and tends to appear in an idealized, often anthropomorphic form. To contact the HGA of the Abra-Melin system is a fairly simple task. The whole system can be summed up in the words: 'invoke often' and 'inflame thyself in prayer'. To attain the 'knowledge and conversation of the HGA', the mage is advised to retire from the world. In a secluded place, the mage prays to the HGA, that the said entity may appear and reveal itself. During the first month, this is done once daily. In the second, twice. This schedule is kept up until the mage spends the entire day dedicating her or himself to the protection and communion of the angel. Of course, this sort of yoga is apt to produce all sorts of madness. By the time the angel reveals itself, the mage will have become so thoroughly purified that s/he is in excellent condition to come to terms with the angel. Equally, the months of steady discipline and burning enthusiasm will ensure the manifestation of a fully fledged angel radiant with power and sentience of the finest kind. It might be claimed that in the Abra-Melin system, the mage creates an angel to radiate true will, while the angel creates an adept fit for the task of living this true will. The appearance of the angel, by the way, is in itself part of the message: the angel symbolizes the true, and previously unknown, will of the adept.

The Abra-Melin system is not the only one that proposes the existence of guardian spirits. In German and Nordic mythology, people knew that they were accompanied by an invisible beast-spirit called the 'Fylgia' (from 'to follow' as the Fylgia follows you around, and vice versa.) Some Fylgia that we know of did appear as wolves, bears, lynx, dragons, eagles or lions. These beasts were the guardians of their human associates. In times of danger, they could be relied upon to give advice, be it through visions, dreams, omina, ritual possession or some sort of divination. The Fylgia, though they could be somewhat wild or mad, were known to have much deeper wisdom than their human counterparts.

Some Fylgia were wise in magick and spell-crafting, allowing them to work synchronicities and other miracles. In times of war, some Fylgia would overwhelm and possess their human friends. 'Going beserk' refers to the old and honourable custom of being possessed by a Fylgia in fighting rage. In such trance-states, ordinary human consciousness would be flooded in a tide of beastly rage and violence, leaving no space for the squeaky little ego to doubt, despair or flee. Berserkers (meaning 'in bear skins') were famed for their wildness, their 'inhuman' reflexes and their ability to endure severe wounds without noticing them.

Chinese martial arts offer another interesting example. Many modern fighting styles evolved out of the ancient Taoist practice 'transform into some beast and find out what happens!' Wu Shu practice involves the motions, behaviour and sentience of such beasts as dragon, tiger, snake, crane, panther, eagle, mantis, deer, spider, bear, tortoise, the

Cat Dance

monkey sage, the swallow, phoenix and countless others. In the old days of shamanistic Taoism, it was common practice to invoke these beasts and to live them, in body, doing dance, ritual and magick. Out of these simple beginnings, hundreds of different styles and techniques were developed. Nowadays many of these systems have become so technical that the joy of animal consciousness has largely been forgotten.

It should be noted that not all beast spirits of Taoism, refer to 'real' beasts. Some of them, such as the dragon, the Qi-Lin, the phoenix or the drunken monkey sage, only exist on the plane of the imagination. They are 'impossible' beasts capable of doing impossible things. People who live with such spirits, as your humble author does, tend to be somewhat paradoxical and crazy. Should you now think that the Wu Shu beasts are only good for fast reflexes and vigorous kicking, you are wrong. Taoism is a life-embracing creed. The beasts often helped in divination, ritual, ceremony and exorcisms, inspired dances, physical exercise, breathing practice, sexual activities and other joys.

These and similar forms of beast-form magick, have largely been forgotten in Western cultures. What remains of the sacred guardian animal is the distorted vision of the eldritch witch with her familiar spirits, toads, frogs, bats, cats, spiders, ravens and the like, and the awful legend of the werewolf, who haunts the forests, howling in fiendish ecstasy. Similar legends of shape-changing (or rather consciousness-changing) can be found in most cultures all over the globe.

Is it natural for humans to develop beast-consciousness? Many children have 'favourite animals' which they love to enact. Try playing 'Tiger' with a child! You may soon find out that it is easier to begin this game than to put a stop to it. This simple little game is very efficient magick (many children's games are pure magick: they program the reality to be), unconscious magick, so natural and enthusiastic that few serious occultists can equal it. You'll be surprised how fully the role is experienced and what amazing powers and drives come to the surface.

Exercise six - waking the beasts

Enough of the theory! Let's get up and do something! How will you wake your beast-spirits? The subconscious mind is no supermarket; you cannot walk in, select a few pets that suit the living room, plus canned food, a solid leash and an insurance certificate. The beasts you'll require will be wild beasts, and wild beasts love to be with wild people. If you are not wild enough you'll end up with an ox, a pig, a sheep or a poodle like so many civil servants do. Considering that so many magicians are rational, reasonable and intellectual scholars, a heady dosage of wildness will do the occult environment a world of good.

The following pattern will help you to send out a call. Feel free to change it as much as you will; what counts is not the technique but the passion you produce. Your task is to call with wildness, emotion and dedication: you can trust your deep mind to work the transformation.

First, you could spend a few hours thinking about what it will be like to live and cooperate with one or more beast spirits. Your conceptions will be wrong, of course, but they will signal your interest. You might aid this process with several methods. You could make a sigil, for instance, asking your deep mind to reveal the beasts to you. You could try to remember all the beasts you loved as a child. You could go into a gentle trance state and ask the deep mind to help you invoke your spirit-guardians. You might pray and offer libations to your ancestors, to the countless generations of life-forms who came before you and whose heritage, encoded in genes, is alive in every cell of you body.

Quite a lot of people do get a contact at this stage. This contact is often a brief and vivid vision or a dream encounter with some animal. Such visions are like gestures. A dweller from the other side says 'Hello!' to you and sends you a visual greeting. This does not mean that you've made it. A real and solid contact requires more commitment, meaning that you'll have to do some work.

1. Preparation

First you'll have to open your reality tunnel (your identity) so that something new might enter. Some easy ways of doing this are confusion, exhaustion and ecstasy. Select a good day for the working. Go out into the country for a long walk. Find a place where you have reasonable privacy and are exposed to the elements. The beast spirits thrive on nature contacts and physical activity, love the howl of the wind, the swiftness of running cross-country, the wideness of the sky, the swaying of the trees and the lust of flesh alive. Such a setting is wonderfully effective, but not essential. If you are good enough you might produce the exhaustion indoors by dancing and sexual activity, but on whole an uncivilized setting makes the calling easier.

2. Find a place that feels good to you.

It doesn't have to be a real wilderness. We once did this working in a public park, and after a time managed to ignore the bewildered people and got good results. In case of emergency you could pretend that you are practising for the annual lunatics' convention. You should feel slightly tired and a little hungry. These are physical sensations that the beasts understand very well. Prepare the place if you feel like it, using a layout of incense and foodstuffs of all varieties. If you like to, you might draw a crossroads or gateway symbol on the ground, using flour or seeds. A little meditation may help to focus the mind.

I would like to add that when you work out in nature, you are a guest. There are a good many esoteric tourists nowadays, who rush from one (supposed) 'place of power' to the next, getting a kick from 'all those ancient energies' and departing without even saying 'thank you'. This sort of thing, as it involves the use of some energy field without respect for its personality, is what I call 'power-site prostitution'. A 'place of power'—and these are far more common than most esoteric tourists suspect—is not simply a battery open for all. Where you find power you will also encounter sentience. This consciousness has been developed by the beings who worked, lived and loved at those sites, by the priests dedicated to them and by the myths and folklore explaining the energies in simple storytelling. When you work your magick at a place of power—even if it is a simple spot where a couple of trees stand, or a little brook dancing through the fields—you would be well advised to say some kindly words to the spirits of the place, before and after your magick. A little prayer and a small offering will tell the nature spirits that you come as a friend.

3. Now for the action.

Pick up a musical instrument, such as a bell, a gong, a tambourine, a drum or a pair of rattles. As you begin to make music, send out your call. It should be fairly easy for you to do so. After all those hours of prayer practice I hope that you are now giving me a superior smile: 'ah, is this all there is to it?' Of course it isn't. Praying to the beast spirits has to be congruent with their animal sentience, otherwise they won't notice the call. Forget about poetic language and subtle definitions. That sort of thing may work well with the more refined gods. It won't work with the beasts. The beasts will react to you emotion, to your passion, to the hunger of the calling. They don't give a damn for the intellectual approach.

I remember an evocation when the caller kept speaking only from the mind. Beautiful words, brilliant and reasonable, well-phrased and a pleasure to behold—but nothing happened. So he increased his effort. Nothing happened. And he kept talking. Then he got angry, and tried to command. Nothing happened. He began to feel like a real fool. Next followed more anger, at being such a fool. When he got really angry, a tiger appeared. Tigers don't care much for reasonable arguments, but anger is something they understand very well.

Perhaps you won't need anger for this working; you can keep your words as simple, crude and repetitive as you feel like; if you feel what you say, there is power in your speech and passion, hunger for union and lust in experience, the beasts will hear and come.

4. Amplify your call

This may take some time, of course. So what do you do? You amplify your call. Keep chanting loudly and passionately. Use your instrument and begin to dance. The trick about this is to dare to be wild. Chant, scream, stomp on the ground, hammer on your drum and keep going.

Keep calling. Imagine how your call radiates, how it unfolds beyond the known universe. Keep calling. Go into exhaustion and get carried away. This is no time for halfhearted gestures; put all your power into it and continue. And continue. You continue with call and dance and noise until you forget about 'feeling strange', until your body shakes, sweat runs down your face and your mind begins to spin.

The power and raw energy you release will attract the beasts. Soon enough you'll find yourself in a loud and hearty shaman's trance. When you feel like it, allow your eyes to close.

5. Keep chanting

Sometime you will begin to see beasts in your imagination. Keep chanting. Some of them will be swift glimpses, others will appear more solid. Let me warn you: some of them will probably be wishful thinking. How do you recognize the real thing? For one thing, wishful thoughts won't be a complete representation, at least during such an expressive trance state. For another, they won't touch strong emotions. If you find yourself observing a beast in a detached intellectual way or notice that ego thinks little greedy thoughts of property and pride, the supposed beast-spirit is not real enough. A real power beast will make your ego squeak, as it will appear much stronger than your conscious mind and threatens to take control. You cannot control such a beast: you will have to come to terms with it.

6. Integration.

It is not enough to confront this brute; you will have to integrate it. I once knew a lady who went through the whole process. She called, and was lucky enough to get a swift response. Through the clouds of incense a bat came for her. The simplest way to integrate a beast is to let it into your body, dancing and enacting it as well as you can. This however, seemed horrible to her. The bat tried to come in and she tried to keep it out. Within moments the dear woman got violently sick and threw up. She hasn't heard of the bat ever since.

There is a certain difference between collecting spirit helpers and collecting stamps. It's not easy to allow a power beast to come in and take control. Our cultural conditioning says that we must stay in control at all costs, however illusionary and restrictive this 'control' may be. Here our cultural imprints are a distinct disadvantage. In other cultures, such as West-Indian Voodoo, ritual possession is approved of and is considered a definite service to society (provided one is 'mounted' by the right sort of spirit). Also, the beasts tend to behave in beastly ways. Some of them may be in a gentle mood but others will upset you considerably. In some shamanic traditions, the beast spirits will introduce themselves by devouring the shaman. Later on they will throw up the bones and bits of carrion, and rearrange them until the shaman comes to life again. This is what I call 'reconstruction of a more appropriate personality'. It's one of the modes of rebirth.

What is it like to enact a beast-form? What is it like when a child pretends to be some beast? Some get going by imagining that the beast enters their body, that inside of this human flesh lurks a savage animal. Then the animal begins to move, begins to run and jump and scream and dance. Others construct a vivid picture, seeing themselves transforming into the beast. This could be a process, it could also be two images superimposed so you can see both of them. When this (dissociated) vision looks very attractive (for example 'large, vivid, clear, colourful, close' and everything else that turns you on), bring it close to yourself and go into it (full association). What does it feel like? Now construct an image showing you even more possessed by that beast. Associate with it. Repeat the process until you feel satisfied.

Sooner or later the beast will move you. This process can be somewhat drastic. Your ego will probably dislike being 'out of control', but as you will have to trust your spirits anyway, you might as well start now. Coordinating beast and human won't be easy either, and perhaps your body will get tossed about a bit. Try to go with it. Human sentience may stay awake provided you don't interfere. The beast will do its will. You may watch, but you may not meddle.

7. Make a pact with the beast

Last, ask the beast whether it agrees to live and work with you. Ask it to cooperate in the great work and aid you in the changes to be. This is an essential step. From now on, the beast will do its best to help you discover and do your true will. It will teach you a lot of new attitudes and methods, new self-aspects will arise and new freedom of choice will widen your reality. Above all, it will reveal that there is much more to yourself than the human personality you believe yourself to be.

8. The time afterwards

In the weeks to follow, you should allow the beast plenty of fun. Frequent transformation and dancing will give strength to the contact and make the trance easier and more elegant. Ask the beast what it likes to do. Find out about its moods and desires, about its ways of problem solving and above all, about its Function, about the things it does for your being as a whole.

This is all I can tell you: experience will reveal the rest. Another vital aspect is this: one beast is not enough. What we need is choice. Though some would-be shamans try to achieve safety by limiting themselves to a single beast, most practising hell-raisers work with several. Some jungle sorcerers in Brasilia chant a whole score of beasts into their belly—each of them a valid way of relating to the world—and mythical European shamans, such as John Doolittle M.D., have done the same with amazing results.

Why limit oneself? If the beasts come freely, you can find out how many you can accommodate. Sure, the first weeks of contact can be pretty wild or even overwhelming. You and your beasts will have to get used to each other, meaning that parts of your personality will be transformed. There will be more choices, more freedom for yourself. The initial exhaustion trance opened the gates and supplied energy for the contact. You won't need such drastic measures once you and your beast have become friends. Soon you will find that the less resistance you produce, the easier cooperation will be. This is not a case of 'either/or' thinking, of being 'either human or beast'. Between these two extremes, there is a wide range of possible and often pleasant, trance states.

I would like to add that beast spirits delight in body. The beasts enjoy to move, to dance, to feast and fuck. If you want to do your beasts a favour, do something good for your body. When I become over-intellectual, and think and talk and write too much, the beasts wake me up. 'Come on', they say, or, if need be, shout, 'Let's go into the woods.'

I hope your beasts will do the same for you.

Joy of Union

Chapter Eleven
Coming to Earth

The themes detailed in *Visual Magick* swiftly passed the realms of 'vision' and 'imagination' to focus on my favourite obsessions, namely the link between the nameless aeons of ancient history, with their tree wisdom, their unique shamanism and their love for direct inspiration via the spirits, and the wordless aeons which are to come, and which refer, quite simply, to what you will make out of these theories and practices. Maybe you enjoyed the techniques, and found them useful to improve the sort of magick which is your will to do. No matter whether you agree or disagree with my ideas, this book will have done its work if it gives you the daring to construct unique new methods of magick to suit your own development and the evolution of the current. One day these new methods may feed others in the current: in feeding others, by the same mouth, we feed ourselves.

In the Maatian system, I believe, we are working hard to avoid the formation of a single tradition. What Maat requires are multiple points of view, which may, or even ought to be, as different as possible. In a wide world full of possible points of view, we do not require a single explanation but a multiple interpretation, just as we have to go beyond a single system, a single dogma or a singular course of attainment which is supposed to satisfy all. Freedom begins with the recognition that in some ways we share the same sort of brain/body/environment structures, while on the other hand each of us is unique.

If you simply imitate what you find on these pages you are doing yourself no good at all. If this book makes you imitate me, you'll perhaps acquire a few technical skills, and this is where it ends. If it allows you to discover your own unique interpretation of visual magick, maybe some day I'll feed on your discoveries. This way the magick stays alive. This leads to a point which is very important to me. What has this book given to you? Have you improved your senses, your imagination, your skills with sigils and trance and prayer? Have you discovered more about the world you created for yourself, and have you made it a better world to live in? Have you discovered more of those self-aspects so commonly hidden to the conscious self?

What do you do with it?

How do you earth your work, your joy, your inspiration? What happens to your visions once you've enjoyed them? How do you express what you experience? You may remember my remarks on earthing excess energies after a working. The simple gesture of falling to the ground, discharging the excess, has several parallels. One gesture will earth energy, another will earth intelligence.

A good many mages and witches use a metaphor to describe their spiritual evolution. They say that they are 'climbing the mountain of initiation', which is supposed to be a hill with many paths leading to a single peak. Be that as it may, the metaphor tends to mislead. In Zen Buddhism, we ask quite seriously: What do you do after you've climbed the thirty foot pole? What do you do after you've climbed one of those mountains of initiations? What do you do when Kundalini has reached the top, when consciousness reaches Kether, when you attain whatever goal you went out for? What do you do after nine long nights atop that windy tree? You can't stay up there forever!

And so we return. Down to earth, bearing the fire from heaven in a single hollow tube. You have learned to receive. Will you learn how to give?

What would happen to your digestion, should you keep stuffing yourself with food while strictly avoiding to go to the toilet once in a while? I know this may sound tasteless, but it's not half as disgusting as what happens to whose witches and mages who keep stuffing themselves with more power, more vision, more joy, more knowledge, more insight, more secrets, more fancy titles, more enlightenment, more grades, more diplomas, more success and more, more, more. When one is always hungry for more food, be it the greater vision, the stronger energy, the true tradition, the absolute orgasm, the ultimate secret or the next-best initiation, one can easily forget one's obligation to the world. Such people suffer from magical constipation, and as they can't let the joy and wonder out in some sensible way, they get clogged, bloated and poisoned by them.

People like to say that they work with this or that current, which may or may not be an adequate description of their work. Often enough, they imply territory and property with the statement. As far as I know, a current is not a thing one can own and sit on, but a state of motion and change. A current is not owned, hoarded and given out in small portions to the faithful. To radiate a current is simply to learn how to become sufficiently empty or absent, so that the current manifests through one's entire personality.

This is hardly practical advice. Remember how power is released into the earth? The same goes for vision, information, realization and intelligence. Intelligence is earthed by communicating it, most often through the medium of art. Art may mean pictures, or words, poetry, writing, sculpture, woodcarving, cooking, musick, or dance, acting, group-experience, festivities, street-theatre and we ought to include the modern art forms as well, such as film-making, installations or computer programming. All these are tools to communicate our experience to others and vice versa. Nema said the following on art and communication:

> *Information sharing can also occur through the practice of art. One virtue of art as a tool in the great work is its ability to move and change an audience through bypassing verbal censors of the unbalanced ego. Art evokes response*

> *from the beholder. A good artist knows precisely which responses he/she wants to evoke, in what order and/or combination; he/she also has the skill to present the proper stimuli to accomplish it. Each medium of art has its particular strengths and weaknesses. . . no matter what the medium, a talented priest can communicate the great fact of our unity without preaching or didacticism. Art shows rather than tells. All great artists function as priests, whether they think of themselves as priests or not.*

Communion through art begins to function once the mage finds some sort of contact to her/his Guardian Angel in Tiphareth and comes to perceive the nature of her/his true will. This will expresses itself through art, and the first work of art of the newborn adept is always her/his own personality. In recognizing our true will, we create personalities for ourselves which can do it. This is called an 'artificial ego', an identity which is specifically designed to do specific things.

The identity you choose to live, the reality you choose to in-dwell, is the most important work of art you'll ever be busy with. Living in accord with your true will demonstrates to the entire world that it is possible and right to do so. Thus you become what Nema calls 'a living talisman for the entire human race.' This is not so much an achievement as an act of dedication. One loves all of oneself, and all that one is or has is put at the disposal of the current. Nor is this act a singular one. Just as there are an infinite number of abysses one can stumble into, so there are an infinite number of personalities one will discover, explore and apply in the doing of one's true will. Truth wears a thousand faces' goes an old saying 'and every single one of them is false'.

To make oneself a 'work of art' is not the end of the process. Every identity one creates for oneself is but one step in the journey. Masks are created, worn and discarded as suits the going. The mask or identity of your childhood became obsolete with the beginning of puberty. The mask of puberty was useless to the adult. As long as life continues, there is no final mask. A mage creates her/his own identity continuously, and doing so, proves that identity and reality can be chosen, and freely made, as suits the love and will of each step of the dance. It's part of the earthing to live in accord with the wealth of our magical visions, and to allow these inner visions to work their transformations in the outer.

The link that bridges the gap between me and you is communication. To move others, we learn what moves us, and communicate the secret to all who are willing to listen. Thus communication becomes a sacrament, a union of intelligence with intelligence. The 'child of the union' is a new state of consciousness.

If you learned to behold visions why not learn to paint them? Allow your inner voices to speak in the outer. Express you inner feelings in dance, posture, gesture, touch and love. Perhaps you can then express what moves you within and reveal your dearest secrets? You will then be sharing your magick with the world

Bibliography

Andreas, C & S, *Change Your Mind and Keep the Change* (Real People Press, MOAB 1987)

Bandler, R *Using Your Brain for a Change* (Real People Press, MOAB 1985)

Bandler, R & Grinder, J *Frogs Into Princes*, *Trance Formations*, *Reframing*, *The Structure of Magic 1 & 2* (Real People Press, MOAB)

Bardon, F *Der Weg Zum Wahren Adepten*, (Bauer Verlag, Freiburg 1956)

Crowley, A *Magick* and everything else

Custor... 'Sigilography' in *Phoenix Rising* Vol 1 No2 (Derby 1982)

Duden #7 Etymologie, (Mannheim 1989)

Edda Translation Simrock, Stuttgart, Cotta 1896

Erickson, M H A *Teaching Seminar with M.H.E.* (Brunner/Mazel NY1980); 'Hypnotic Realities' (NY 1976 with E. Rossi)

Fischer, S 'Blätter von Bäumen' *Zweitausendeins* (Frankfurt 1982)

Frazer, Sir J G *The Golden Bough* (MacMillan, London 1922)

Fries, J, *Helrunar* (Mandrake 1993)

Golther, W, *Handbuch der Germanischen Mythologie* (Magnus, Kettwig 1987)

Grant, K, *The Magical Revival, Images and Oracles of Austin Osman Spare, Nightside of Eden, Aleister Crowley and the Hidden God,*

Cults of the Shadow (Originally published by F Muller but currently being reprinted by Skoob)

Gregorius, G, *Die Mag. Praxis d.* 'Pentagramm Magie' (Fraternitas Saturni, Berlin April 1963)

Halifax, J, *Shamanic Voices* (Penguin 1979)

Holdstock, R, *Mythago Wood* (1984)

Holdstock, R, *Lavondyss* (1988)

Martinie, L, 'Pangenic Occultism' *Cincinnati Journal of Ceremonial Magick* 7, 1989

Martinie, L *Waters of Return* (Black Moon 1986)

Mathers, S L MacGregor, *The Book of the Sacred Magick Of Abra-Melin the Mage* (1901)

Mühlbauer, E, 'Weisheit aus Sand' in *Esotera II* Bauer Verlag (1989)

Nadolni, S Die Entdeckung der Langsamkeit (Piper München)

Nema, 'The Priesthood' *Cincinnati Journal of Magick* 1983 & Black Moon 1985

Oppitz, M, *Schamanen vom Blinden Land*, (Syndikat, Frankfurt 1981)

Paracelsus *Die Geheimnisse* (Dieterich, Leipzig 1941)

Rösing, I, *Dreifaltigkeit und Orte der Kraft Mundo Ankari* Vol II (Greno, Nördlingen 1988)

Rossi, E, *The Psychology of Mind-Body Healing* (Norton, NY 1986)

Saso, M, *The Teachings of Taoist Master* Chuang (Yale University Press 1978)

Sieg, H, *Baum und Strauch dir ewig Heilverbündet* (Rowohlt, Stuttgart 1939)

Spare, A O, *Book of Pleasure, Focus of Life, Automatic Drawing.*

Springer, S, 'Left Brain, Right Brain' *Scientific American* (1984)

Note: For a good demonstration of 'Beast-form' Kung Fu, see The Snake in the Eagles Shadow starring Jackie Chan (available on video)

Index

D

E

Y

Z

Lightning Source UK Ltd.
Milton Keynes UK
UKHW010831140121
376915UK00001B/9